12/01

Born to Fly

THE HUMP

A WWII Memoir

by

Dr. Carl Frey Constein

Copyright © 2001 by Dr. Carl Frey Constein

This book may not be reproduced in any form without the written consent of the author.

ISBN# 1-58500-643-2

This book is printed on acid free paper.

1stbooks rev. 2/6/01

Thanks To

Anne & Millie
my favorite editors and consultants

. . . and to

**a couple dozen friends and several
pilots who read the manuscript
and made valuable suggestions.**

CHINA - BURMA - INDIA THEATER

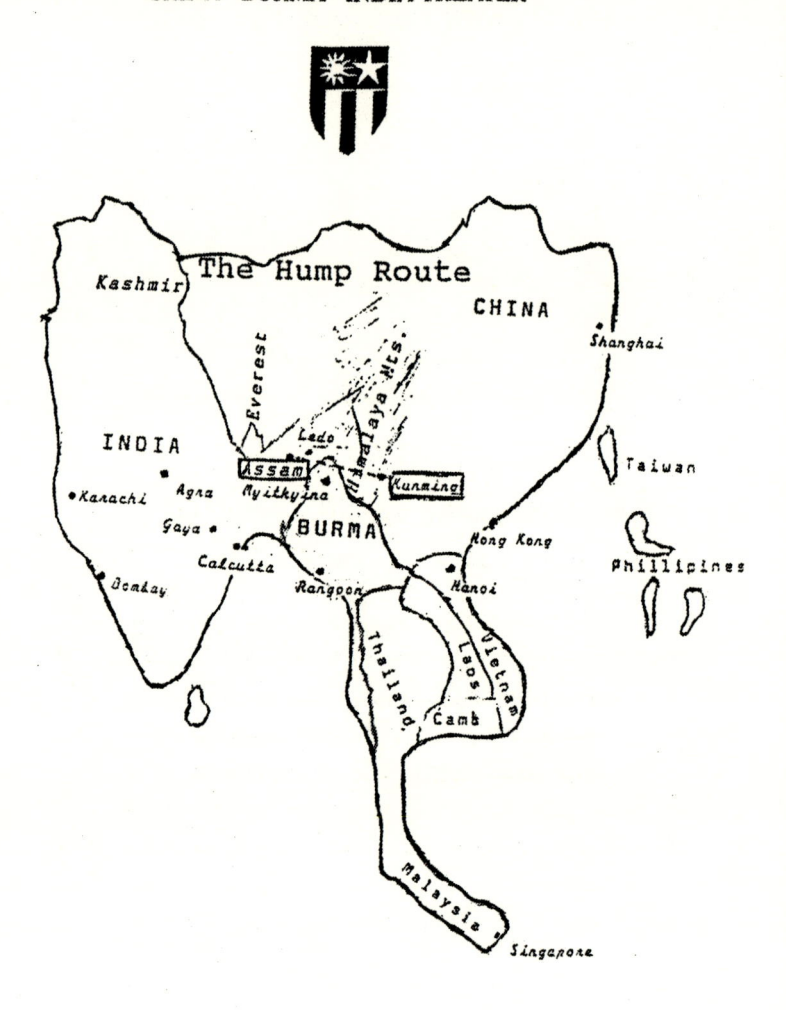

CONTENTS

Preface v

1 First Flight 1
2 Greetings from the President 7
3 Skinny Me an MP? 17
4 Solo! 24
5 The Dreaded E Ride 31
6 "It's a Long, Long Way" 37
7 Flight to Nowhere 46
8 "I Will Life Up Mine Eyes" 51
9 What's It All About? 60
10 A Rough December 71
11 The Worst Day 80
12 Visiting Mighty Everest's Cousins 90
13 Of Nudes and Seals 97
14 The Taj Mahal Caper 106
15 Guests of the Maharajah 112
16 The Whole Tooth 119
17 Going Home 127
   Epilogue 132

Preface

Hear the word *airlift,* and *Berlin* pops into your mind. But there was a World War II predecessor to the famous Berlin airlift, smaller but infinitely more daring, more dangerous. It was called the Hump. For nearly a year I flew this five-hundred-mile route from India to China across the Himalaya Mountains.

The war ended and I came home, eager to get to work, to make a life, to chase my favorite phantoms. Like twelve million other veterans, I was too busy for war stories. Now, a thousand of us die every day; the meter is running. Some old soldiers are battle-scarred and want to forget, sharing their memories, if at all, with only their families. I had a few terrifying experiences of my own, but I have no difficulty calling them up.

None of the forty-seven men and women whose accounts Tom Brokaw relates in his bestseller, *The Greatest Generation,* served in China-Burma-India, the CBI. That theater of war and the Hump itself rate a mere footnote in military history. Yet, at the time, *Life Magazine* called it the most dangerous non-combat flying in the war, the world's worst weather over the world's highest mountains. More than five hundred planes crashed, most on the high peaks of China. Thirteen hundred pilots and crew were killed, some dying horrible, lingering deaths after bailing out into the Burmese jungle. Saddest of all, some crews took off one day in India, headed east, and were never heard from again. I wasn't smarter than those pilots. I wasn't braver. I was luckier.

Brokaw has urged us to tell our stories. Mine is about a small-town boy who grew up during the Great Depression, took a circuitous route to aviation cadets, trained on the C-46, then flew ninety-six round-trips across the Hump.

What was it like? It was challenging and frightening. At times it was just plain boring. But on those rare flights when the day was crystal clear and the night starry, the awesome beauty of the mountains soothed a pilot's soul.

First Flight

I was seven in 1927 when Lucky Lindy coaxed his Spirit of St. Louis across the vast, forbidding Atlantic. Six years later I "slipped the surly bonds of earth" to take my first flight. How could I know that one day I would make my own tiny blip in aviation history?

My maiden flight came when I was twelve. One bright summer morning a barnstormer buzzed our town of Fleetwood, Pennsylvania, in his World War I surplus biplane. When we were sure he was going to land, my friends and I dropped our baseball gloves, hopped on our bikes and pedaled furiously out onto the highway. It took us fifteen long minutes to get to George Schuler's farm. Sure enough, there the beauty was, sitting benignly in the field near the highway, the rugged pilot busy posting his sign: "Airplane Rides $1.00." We pedaled back home like greased lightning to beg for the dollar.

In 1933 a dollar bought a world of goodies -- a half-dozen admissions to the movies, a couple weeks' supply of Hershey bars. Hard times or not, Mother knew every kid needed a little pin money. I'd approach her, not Father.

Father was an upholsterer at the Fleetwood Metal Body Company. He used to scare me half to death whenever he re-covered furniture at home and threw a handful of tacks into his mouth, retrieving them one by one with his magnetic tack hammer. Fleetwood was *the* place for the rich and famous to have custom bodies made for their high-priced chassis -- Packard, Mercedes, La Salle, Rolls-Royce, Stuts, Cadillac, Dusenberg. Among the customers were the Vanderbilts, Rockefellers, and Mellons, U.S. Presidents and European princes, and silent film stars Mary Pickford and

Rudolph Valentino. If you'd like to own Rudy's 1926 Fleetwood-bodied Isotta Franschini, it's for sale in Danville, California -- at a reported one million six!

In 1930 Fisher Body acquired the company and moved it to Detroit, urging Fleetwood's four hundred skilled craftsmen to move with them. Pennsylvania Germans, these men lived their lives, as their parents and grandparents before them, surrounded by some of the richest soil and most beautiful farmland in the world. They were not about to uproot their families; not one moved.

Ultimately, Fleetwood made its mark in automobile history. In honor of the acquired company's supreme quality, General Motors named its top-of-the-line Cadillac the "Fleetwood." The model was discontinued in 1996, but every now and then I hear GM may bring it back. Until then, I'll hang onto my mint-condition 1990 navy blue beauty, a baby clone of the Presidential armored limo.

I hadn't intended to buy a new car that year, but to soften the blow when my wife's Alzheimer's forced her to give up driving, I offered to trade up the family car to whatever she wanted. She chose a Cadillac; in honor of Father, I chose a Fleetwood.

I was nine when the stock market crashed. As though the town hadn't been hit hard enough, the Great Depression rode in like the Black Horseman of the Apocalypse. I picture Mother nervous as a cat as she went about doing the weekly wash on that first Monday of 1933 -- something about President Roosevelt closing the banks. Think of my parents' fears -- little money in the house, five mouths to feed, no job, no income of any kind, no Social Security.

I remember Mother's kindness -- and courage -- in giving me money for treats, for the movies, and especially for an airplane ride. Father groused about it for a week. He was a stern, taciturn, frugal "real" German. I believe he loved us three children, but he seldom showed it. Both in their second marriages, my parents must have been happier in their first, I came to believe. Financial problems aggravated their uneasy relationship, but at least they were spared every family's greatest Depression fear -- losing their home. Thanks to Mother's first husband, our large, comfortable house was mortgage-free.

We kids didn't know better: we grew up with our fun and interests, including airplanes. I was not one of those lads who scanned the sky whenever they detected the faint buzz of a propeller biting the air. I recall playing pilot only once. On the second floor of their father's garage, Robert Angstadt and his brother Danny fashioned a wooden cockpit surrounded by truncated wings and a fuselage. Two discarded Atwater-Kent radio chassis provided a great instrument panel. I joined their Walter Mitty flying high jinks but soon lost interest. Not the Angstadt boys. After service in the Air Corps, they went on to make careers of aviation, flying and servicing helicopters in St. Louis and later managing a helicopter service in Chicago.

John Schach, another friend who was crazy about flying, got to live his dream. From his base in Tezgaon, India, he flew fifty-eight round-trip flights over the Hump in C-54s.

And there was Carl Erdman, an octogenarian friend who never outgrew his love of flying. Until his recent death, he continued to commute, solo, between Reading and his summer home in New Hampshire in his Piper Aztec.

I too enjoyed flying, but it wasn't in my blood as it was in my friends'. Still, I look back fondly on that first flight. I can see the barnstormer's scarf and scuffed helmet. I gasped when I caught an aerial view of my hometown and the green and brown stripes and patches of fields which hemmed it in. It was a colorful painting, a miniature Christmas village -- the sprawling, deserted body works and nearby railroad station, the silos at Uncle Wes's mill, the church with its cemetery tucked in, the orderly grid of streets, the colorful spectacle of summer gardens, the mosaic of red, black, and silver roofs. I pointed down when I spotted my house -- as though the pilot cared. Looking up, I saw the vast sky, a blue tent in the heavens, fringed with a host of angelic clouds. What would it be like to fly into those giant cotton balls?

When I became an aviation cadet, I found out. Flying in and out of a covey of fluffy cumulus in a PT-19 was peaceful, sublime. I soon discovered it wasn't speed or aerobatics that thrilled me, it was again the joy of seeing beauty spread beneath my wings. On commercial flights here and there since the war, I've been overwhelmed by the spectacular views the world offers from 30,000 feet. And always, to dream: what are the people like who live there in the Sahara Desert, in the frozen lands of the North, in Africa's Serenghetti? And over the Hump, the Naga headhunters, the peaceful Kachins, the Chinese living in villages precariously perched on mountainsides a mile or more above sea level.

Every flight, every view, even on mundane commercial routes, offers visual delights. I'm perplexed when I see blasé passengers ignoring the marvelous sights, preferring instead to sleep or fiddle with their electronic devices.

Growing up, I enjoyed everything except hobbies. I didn't collect stamps, and I didn't build models. I tackled my first one when a C-46 model finally came out years after the war. I was a big kid then, over fifty. Inexperienced, inept, I botched the job terribly. The wounded whale was relegated to fly the calm skies over the ping-pong table in the seldom-used game room. My second effort, while not perfect, at least looks airworthy, good enough for the family room.

The C-46 Commando is a smooth, rounded airplane, the fuselage a bit like a whale, in fact. It's more attractive than the Douglass C-47 Gooney Bird with its broken nose and squared-off tail. If they were automobiles, the C-46 would be in the Cadillac showroom; the C-47 would be out on the used-car lot. The Commando was chosen for the Hump not because of its beauty but because of its four-ton payload and its power, its ability to fly high and thumb its nose at the lofty peaks of the Himalayas. But the Douglass outclasses the C-46 in dependability and longevity -- two thousand C-47s or DC-3s still flying throughout the world. Not bad for used cars. I believe there are only two C-46s operational in the states, their glory days on the Hump long past.

The Hump -- no other place in the world like it. I wonder who gave it that name. It may have been the China National Aviation Corporation (CNAC) pilot who in December of 1941 chartered a route in a DC-3 and proved the feasibility of supplying China by air. Exactly three years later I was flying his course. I had some scary moments during some of my ninety-six round-trips, but even so, flying the Hump was the perfect assignment for a guy so keen on observing beauty from the air. If I was born to fly, I was born to fly the Hump.

But that would come eleven years after my first flight. Meanwhile, my life would be filled with the storm and stress of adolescence, with school and college, and with work.

Greetings from the President

I suppose psychologists today would say I had an impoverished childhood. If I did, I never knew it. I had my tennis, my bicycle for cowboys and Indians, my baseball; Mush Schlegel and I set our traps for muskrats; and, when I could squeeze an extra fifteen cents out of Mother, I indulged in a chocolate-marshmallow-peanut sundae, the famous CMP, to go with a cherry Coke after the movies.

The Saturday night movie was the highlight of the week. My friends and I got in line early at the Fire Company Auditorium Theater for a good seat. If we could persuade girls to join us (of course they had to pay their own way), we sat in the balcony for a little necking.

The Fox-Pathé News of the World was followed by not one but two serials like The Lone Ranger or Popeye the Sailor Man. But the best fun was the jeering and shouting and stamping of feet when the film tore during the feature and the theater went dark. The longer it took to rethread the projector, the more raucous we became, pausing only in our reveling to tease any teary-eyed girls if the tears came at a tender moment.

My family didn't own a car. A couple times a year Mother took us shopping in Reading, a thriving city of one hundred thousand, and the county seat. We'd take the trolley car, later the bus. We never missed going to the city at Christmastime, country folk gawking at spectacular streetlights on Penn Street and elaborate displays in Pomeroy's and Whitner's department stores.

Our lives revolved around school -- one building, grades one (no kindergarten) through twelve. Through the years, only one new pupil joined our class of 1938, and no one dropped out. We were peas in a pod -- thirty-eight kids in the same class for nine years, then splitting into either the academic or business course. We must have been very, very good. Not all the girls were virgins, but I recall only one who became pregnant and dropped out. All of us boys had our problems with girls.

The school ground was our place to hang out in the summertime. Even on rainy days, we were "back at school."

Hard times dragged on. I still can't see how my parents put food on the table, especially in the early thirties. I recall so clearly our spartan nights -- only one light on in the living room. But in his cultured tones, FDR promised us in a Fireside Chat we had nothing to fear but fear itself. In one hundred days, Congress passed his New Deal -- Emergency Banking Act, Emergency Relief Act, National Recovery Administration, Works Progress Administration (WPA), Social Security.

The hoopla that went with these programs was contagious, even in small-town America. When I drive through Fleetwood, I see myself in white shirt and pants and white bucks (and hear the screeches from my clarinet), an eighth grader proudly marching with the FHS band down Main Street in the NRA parade, banners everywhere announcing the coming of a new day.

Uncle Sam became the nation's primary employer. Men hired to build walls or repair roads found themselves in a work climate quite different from the profit-driven employment of their former jobs. They began loafing. Everywhere in the land "We poke along" became the WPA's mantra.

The public works job in Fleetwood was removal of unused trolley tracks. Father was hired as a timekeeper. A proud man, he must have been a pariah for expecting the men to actually put in eight hours of real work.

I will be forever grateful to my father for a golden gift -- the gift of music. He was a superb tenor, a church soloist in Lancaster County, where he'd lived before he married the widow Clara Brown and moved into her house in Fleetwood. By the time I was born, he was no longer singing regularly; I heard him only twice. His voice and his singing technique, I knew even then, were magnificent. He loved opera.

Few families had radios, but, surprisingly, we did. It was a cabinet Radiola 18, powerful enough to pull in KDKA out of Pittsburgh. Every Sunday night we eagerly awaited the concert of the Ford Symphony Orchestra, again reading the printed program we received in the mail.

Actually, the week's musical highlight always came a day earlier. Father reveled in the Saturday matinee Texaco broadcasts of the Metropolitan Opera. I began listening too, until I reached sixteen, when I clerked all day Saturday in the A&P store. I can still hear the mellifluous tones of announcer Milton Cross describing massive elephants crossing the stage of the old Met in the Triumphal March in *Aida.*

Through the years I've pondered about that expensive radio. Why, if we had so little, did we have it? How could we afford to buy it? I believe Father skimped for years to purchase the one thing that brought him his only real joy -- music. I'm glad he did. My brother, George, became a cellist, and I've had a life-long love affair with classical music.

I'm grateful, too, for the friendship of Dr. Gehris and his family, next door neighbors, for extending my love of music to orchestral music. Starting in eighth grade, they invited me to join them for Sunday afternoon concerts of the Reading Symphony Orchestra. What a thrill to catch sight of Hans Kindler, conductor of the National Symphony Orchestra, gliding in from the wings then raising his baton. What a thrill to hear Jose Iturbi, Walter Gieseking, Zino Francescotti, Giovanni Martinelli!

Too late I thought about getting their autographs; I was probably too shy to approach them anyway. An idea popped into my head. I wrote to my favorites and asked them to sign and return the postcards I'd enclosed. They occupy a special place on my family room wall. I cherish most Serge Koussevitsky, conductor of the Boston Symphony Orchestra, and the super stars of a bygone era of grand opera -- Kirsten Flagstadt, Lauritz Melchoir, Lawrence Tibbett, Lily Pons.

My other big interest was reading. My favorite books were Emerson's essays, the novels of Jeffrey Farnol, and the adventures of Richard Halliburton, who claimed in *Royal Road to Romance* to have swum in the reflecting pool at the Taj Mahal. Years later I discovered firsthand that only fish can swim in that shallow pool.

I liked history and kept a scrapbook of articles about world leaders and events. Germany cried for "lebesraum," Japan claimed its "place in the sun." The war clouds gathered. I stayed after class to discuss the developments with Dave Zimmerman, my favorite teacher. I became convinced we could not remain isolated from a world about to be engulfed in war.

George Messerschmidt, Fleetwood's most prominent citizen, was as close to the European tinderbox as an American could get: United States Consul General in Berlin. Knowing he was home to visit his mother, I watched for him to strut by with his cane and homberg. When I saw him approach, I rushed to him for an autograph, my first.

Few of us FHS seniors gave thought to war or what we'd be doing after graduation. My brother was enrolled at nearby Kutztown State Teachers College. I assumed I'd be going to work; it just wasn't in the cards for me to go to college. But Mother was a magician. She squirreled away enough money and insisted that I too enroll at Kutztown. From tenth grade on, I'd worked weekends at the grocery store, and mowed, it sometimes seemed, half the lawns of Fleetwood. So I had saved a bit of money on my own.

Not that Kutztown was expensive. Beyond a contingency fee of seventy-two dollars and very low tuition, most of which I worked off in a student-assistance program, I had no expenses. Hard to believe, isn't it? Of course, living at home saved the big expense, college room and board.

If I hadn't been such a straight arrow, I could have had an even better deal. Like my father, I was a tenor, singing in the choirs of both the Reformed and Lutheran congregations in St. Paul's Union Church next door. With Pennsylvania German frugality, the two congregations had built and shared one church building. Try that today! The Board of Elders of the Lutheran congregation took a liking to me and offered me a four-year full-tuition scholarship, room and board included, to prestigious Muhlenberg College in Allentown -- if I agreed to go on to the seminary after graduation to become a minister. Call me stupid. Call me naive. I never even considered accepting the offer then reneging on my promise and following another career. Nor would my friends.

How simple our morality was. In those innocent years no one could have conceived of truth spinning, moral relativism, Orwellian revisionism. Who could have believed that years later our Commander-in-Chief would be charged with lying under oath and obstructing justice, would be impeached, and would say that impeachment wasn't so bad. As a veteran, as an American, I am deeply offended and saddened by the President's conduct and low moral standards.

So, back in those simpler days, I enrolled in Kutztown State Teachers College, thanks to my mother and her love for me. About Kutztown we used to say in good humor, if you can't go to college, go to Kutztown.

The college had its fifteen minutes of national glory, dubious though it was. One Monday in the fall of my freshman year in 1938, I drove to Kutztown in my run-down 1929 Chevy coupe and joined other commuters in our "den". Swallowing goldfish was the college craze. The record was something like fifty fish.

"Hell, that's nothing," freshman Howard Francis said. "I can beat that." We took him up on his boast, chipped in to buy several bowls of sunnies and escorted him to Tumbler's Tavern, a block from the campus. The guy meant it. He swallowed a dozen in the first couple minutes. The word spread, and soon Tumbler's was jammed with cheering students eager to witness history in the making. After he got to fifty-one, a roar erupted from the raucous spectators. But Francis wasn't finished. To make certain his record would stand, he downed a dozen more. He made only one request: a salt shaker. That night, Lowell Thomas, the Walter Cronkite of early radio, announced the new record.

Meanwhile, the world was teetering on the brink. In my sophomore year, Germany blitzkrieged into Poland and the war in Europe was on. Nazi Stuka bombers and panzer divisions proved invincible. America had already begun building up its defenses, factories working around the clock to turn out ships, tanks, guns, and planes for its own arsenal and for lend-lease to England. The war was pulling the economy out of the Great Depression. The Fleetwood Craftsmen Company, headed by former Fleetwood Body principals, was making seventy percent of the hammocks for Navy ships, coincidentally in the old auto body building. In college, in town, everywhere, army khakis and navy blues were showing up.

In my junior year, I sat behind Amy Gring, a pretty freshman, at a KSTC football game at Albright Stadium. We dated and fell in love. Every Saturday night after I finished work at the A&P, and every Sunday afternoon, I drove to her home in Reading in my old Chevy, my B gasoline sticker on the back window.

I'd bought the Black Widow about fourth-hand, I figured. It was sporty enough -- it had a rumble seat -- and cheap enough, but it needed a lot of work. It gobbled a quart of oil with every tank of gas. Leaks around the windshield and gaps under the doors made it a sunny-day-only car. You could see the road beneath the passenger-side door. The beauty had no radio, of course, and no heater. On

Saturday nights, exhausted from working twelve hours, I struggled to stay awake as I drove the fifteen miles home from Amy's. I sang arias at the top of my voice, put one leg under the other on the seat, even talked to myself. More than once I woke with a start when my right wheels hit the berm.

Amy and I went to the movies frequently with her best high school friend, Gerry Mellinger. Dick, her husband, was eager to go into aviation cadets and tried to persuade me to join him. Unduly envious of Gus Riemondi and Penny Adams showing off their officers' uniforms on the streets of Fleetwood, I too wanted an officer's commission. But I leaned toward the Army. If I could wait until I had my degree, I thought I'd have a good crack at Officers' Training School (OCS).

In my senior year in college, Japan bombed Pearl Harbor, and the world changed forever. Used to the ubiquitous "Made in Japan" junk, we woke up to a new Japan. We stomped our cigarette butts on Tojo's teethy smile peering at us from our Jigg's ash stands.

Americans over sixty-five will tell you exactly where they were when they heard the news that fateful Sunday in December. I was on my way to visit Amy and heard the news at a gas station. Fascinated by connections, I later discovered that on this same day a CNAC pilot was charting an air route over the Himalayas, a Hump route for me to fly.

Three months later my family took a severe hit: Father had a stroke, paralyzed completely on his right side. I took his place as a cutter at the Craftsmen, working on the night shift, student-teaching during the day. I continued working there after I graduated from Kutztown.

When the company was awarded the Navy E for Excellence, the townspeople were invited to the Fire Company Auditorium to share in the honor. Management asked me to accept the award for the employees and later invited me to travel to New York with them for the annual meeting of the National Association of Manufacturers. I recall how excited I was to hear the speaker, Edward J. Stettinius, secretary of state, and to inhabit, if only for a day, that lofty, sophisticated world in the ballroom of the Waldorf Astoria.

Back home, down to earth again, what I wanted more than anything else in life was to put on an officer's uniform. No boy in Fleetwood could have been more eager to go to war. Most of my friends were already in the service; a few were officers. A few, like Paul Schlegel, Navy air ace in the Battle of Midway, were war heroes. I wanted an officer's commission so badly I could taste it. Then I heard bad news: all Officer Candidate Schools were closed. I was crushed.

My brother was drafted into the Army. We put a star in the window, and I became the family's main support. Working in a defense industry, I could have sat out the war. The final straw was the boring, no-brain job of cutting six layers of mattress ticking, folding individual cuts and carrying them to the sewers' pile. Eight hours a day, day after day. I had to get out.

But before I could leave home, I had to reckon with my straight-arrow conscience. A private's pay was fifty dollars a month. GIs with dependents could have twenty-eight dollars deducted and sent home. The Army added twenty-two dollars to the dependent's stipend. My brother was doing that. I'd do the same, and together our contributions would supplement Father's disability payment. That left twenty-two dollars a month for me.

Okay, so I couldn't go to OCS and become a ninety-day wonder. I'd just have to take my chances. I asked the Draft Board to call me up as soon as possible. In December, a year after Pearl Harbor, just in time for it to be a Christmas card, I received my Selective Service "Greetings" from President Roosevelt.

New Year's Day, 1943, marked the start of a new life. I was sworn into the United States Army. Mother put another star in the window.

Skinny Me an MP?

I said goodbye to my Black Widow. America's mighty war industry devoured all the steel it could get; I sold her for scrap. Fifty dollars!

Saying goodbye to my sweetheart was tougher, bringing on a gush of tears. They were not Amy's alone. I was shocked and embarrassed. I'd thought of myself as stoic, dauntless; now I felt fragile and vulnerable. Perhaps it was overwork, I rationalized, or the strain I was under in my family, perhaps a subconscious fear of danger or of being away from home. Except for a few one-day visits to New York City and the Jersey shore, I'd never even been out of the state. An innocent abroad in the service was what I'd soon be.

The next day, a busload of sad sack draftees left Berks County for the sprawling New Cumberland Army Classification Center near Harrisburg. Terrified, I stepped off the bus, my first step in a new life.

Half paralyzed from fright, our motley crew was marched double-time to the mess hall, the sergeant shouting inexplicable orders. The meal of the day, rubberized meatloaf, stayed with me all of five minutes. Then, amid jeers and whistles from every GI we passed, we were herded to the quartermaster. Corporals and sergeants tossed me shirts, pants, jackets as I answered their loud queries: waist? -- 30;

chest? -- 36; neck? -- 14. Without recognizing the symbolism, I cast off my civies and put on my new life, starting with the ugliest looking OD underwear ever seen on the face of the earth.

The Army wasn't tailor-fussy about how my clothes fit, but shoes? That was different. I stepped down from the platform staring at my shiny 9 AAs. "They feel fine, Sarge," I said.

"Don't fit," he growled. "Report back to the barracks."

I was there -- in New Cumberland, not in the barracks -- two months awaiting special-order 9 AAAs! Friends who sloshed over the battlefields of France and Germany in ill-fitting boots still don't believe me. Whose army were you in? they ask. Shuffling back to the barracks after dinner, small yellow tags still stapled to every part of my overcoat, I was greeted along the way with "Yardbird" -- the lowest of the Army's low.

Winter in New Cumberland was frigid, a near record. On outside detail, assigned to load and unload supplies from the back of a truck, I came down with the most severe cold of my life and reported to sick bay. In spite of a death-rattle cough from deep within my bronchial tubes, the medics sent me packing without medication. Two weeks later I finally got a pass home and immediately went to see Dr. Gehris next door. I spent the weekend in bed.

At New Cumberland I was introduced to Army life -- dog tags, VD films, shots, chow call, and the fabled short-arm inspection. I became acquainted with the types of men I'd run into again and again -- the loud-mouths, the cheats, the phonies, the goof-offs, the jokesters, the losers, the scoundrels and scum Shakespeare compared to dogs. "Aye, in the catalogue ye go for men."

Born to Fly the Hump

A buddy from college who was working in the classification office told me I'd soon be shipped to an MP battalion in Philadelphia. Me a policeman? God! Ralph Waldo Emerson had taught me the law of compensation: at least I'd be close to home, I'd be able to see Amy some weekends. A week or so later, someone must have noticed my education. I was pulled off outside detail to work in the office. Big deal.

Late one Saturday I was given an overnight leave.

I got to Fleetwood at midnight. Early Sunday morning I took a bus to Reading. Amy called jeweler Bill Diller, who met us at his store on Schuylkill Avenue so we could pick out a ring. We were engaged.

In another couple weeks a truckload of us left for Philadelphia. The verdant Belmont Plateau in the city's Fairmount Park became the base for the 722nd MP Battalion. I called Amy to tell her where I was, being careful not to reveal my top secret military mission, guarding the coal piles of the Philadelphia Electric Company!

From the start, something didn't seem right about this outfit. I realized what it was: all the recruits were either hard of hearing or had bad vision, or both. I was in a limited service outfit. My disability? Underweight from my half-year trauma at home, I weighed only one hundred fifteen pounds. After a few weeks of regular hours and meals, I was back up to my fighting weight of one hundred thirty pounds, the only 1-A GI in the outfit!

Most of the men in my barracks were West Virginia ridge-runners who talked as though they had mush in their mouths. But they were good guys, guys with names like Kresinski and Pistininzzi.

Not everyone in the barracks was a hillbilly. Assigned to the bunk next to mine was Dick Holland, a Philadelphian. We hit it off immediately and have been lifelong friends. Music one of our common interests, one night we got a leave to hear the famous Philadelphia Orchestra. I was thrilled to be in the old Academy of Music and hear for the first time a composition I love, Berlioz's *Symphonie Fantastique*.

Leaves were few and far between. The 722nd must have been the most chickenshit outfit in the US Army. You would have thought what we were being trained to do ranked with battleground warfare itself. I hated it, hated the Army. The thirteen weeks of basic training were hell, mostly because the officers and non-coms were so damned solemn, so grouchy, so lacking in basic humanity.

At last, basic training with its forced marches in the rain came to an end, and the 722nd took on its mission of guarding coal piles. I wondered who guarded the electric plants at Grays Ferry Avenue and Norristown before we got there. I was assigned to D Company, with Captain Slattery the CO and Sergeant Nuckles the first sergeant. They stayed up nights planning how they could be obnoxious.

The duty went like this. A platoon was assigned to walk guard duty at a power plant for twelve hours, each MP on duty three hours, then off the next three. Boring, boring, boring. I can't describe how much I hated it. Think of it, three hours of walking in front of a coal pile with a gun on your shoulder, no stopping, no sitting, nobody to be seen. It was hell, especially at night.

My five months at Belmont Plateau were terrible. Of course there was a war on. Of course we had a job to do. But couldn't we all lighten up a bit, especially after basic training? My 722nd memory bank carries only one comical incident.

A spanking new second lieutenant was brought into D Company. At least he could smile. Conscientious and eager, he decided one Friday night to go all out with our platoon and have toe-nail inspection! I doubt that you'll find that in any Army manual. He had us clip our nails then sit on the edge of our bunks as he made his way around to inspect. One GI who knew about such things got up his nerve and told him that straight across the toe, not rounded, was the proper way. The ninety-day wonder thought a moment then issued a remarkable military countermand: "As you were, men."

My most vivid, most embarrassing memory of the 722nd is of leaving Philadelphia's 30th Street Station one day for a five-day encampment. We were loaded down with two full duffel bags, ready to fight in the torrid Tropics or the far reaches of the frigid North. My bags were so heavy I simply couldn't get them up to my shoulders. Face flushed, I dragged them down the stairs and through the cavernous station!

Captain Slattery was the prototype chickenshit CO. Other companies got weekend passes; D company got four-hour passes. At least Amy and I could spend pleasant Sunday afternoons in Fairmount Park and downtown Philadelphia.

On days we were not on guard duty, D company pulled other detail, like KP. Surprisingly, peeling potatoes wasn't so bad compared to a far worse detail, tending the smoky pot-bellied coal stoves in the platoon's barracks all night long.

I was frustrated. I'd given up a boring civilian job for a boring Army job that paid ten times less. Not too smart. I had to get out of this outfit. I had to. Walking guard duty one pitch black night at the Norristown plant, I gazed up and spotted a plane high overhead. In a flash, it came to me! I'd apply for aviation cadets.

Between tours the next day I went to Captain Slattery's office. I expected some of his chickenshit to hit the fan. Did it ever!

"Absolutely not!" he shrieked. "Permission denied. Get the hell out of here!"

Head down, I traipsed back to the barracks and plopped down on the bunk.

An idea struck. I sat up. I'd visit the recruiting office downtown and see if anything could be done.

I could hardly wait for Saturday to come. Dick noticed my fidgeting. "You seem a bit nervous, Carl," he said. "You okay?"

I filled him in on my plans.

After the Saturday morning formation, I took a bus downtown to the Army Air Corps recruiting office. Yes, the sergeant assured me, aviation cadet training was the highest priority. All organizations were under orders to release personnel who wished to apply.

A few days later Slattery called me in. I stood at attention. "Constein," he barked, "I can't stop you from leaving, but you sure as hell better not wash out of cadets." He sprang up from his desk and strode to me, still standing at attention. In my face, he yelled, "If you wash out, I'll have your ass back here so fast you won't know what hit you. Dis - missed!"

I left his office, motivated to succeed in cadets, one might say.

A week later the orders arrived, with a bonus -- a seven-day leave before reporting to Goldsboro, North Carolina. Dick got permission to accompany me to the 30th Street Station, a place I wanted to erase from memory.

I felt bad for Dick, so much talent wasted in that terrible outfit. But when we met after the war, he didn't complain about the 722nd. A native Philadelphian, he told me with pride that Belmont Plateau was restored to its original beauty, and that the site had been considered as permanent home of the United Nations, losing out to New York City.

I boarded the train for Reading's Franklin Street Station. I sat back and closed my eyes, dreaming of seven whole days at home with the girl I loved.

Solo!

Again Amy and I said a long goodbye, not tearfully this time, for we knew where I'd be and what I'd be doing. At the Outer Station she gave me one last precious kiss before I stepped onto the Reading Railroad's local to Philadelphia.

I arrived at the Broad Street Station and boarded a troop train for a better life in the Air Corps. Late at night we arrived in Goldsboro.

Almost immediately, I felt at home south of the Mason-Dixon Line -- the sandy soil, the pine trees, the barracks and PX, the good chow, the guys, the King Cotton Hotel. Everything except the heat. I drank Cokes like water.

I sensed a new spirit here -- more relaxed, better morale, more on the ball, a difference of night and day between the Air Corps and the Army. I dreaded having to take basic training again, but, except for the monster obstacle course, it was a snap.

My second time around, basic training and the military mystique struck my funny bone. All over America, I wrote Amy, millions of men were marching up and down the field, hup ... 2 ... 3 ... 4, learning their left foot from their right, doing push-ups and jump-ups and sit-ups, even learning to dispatch the enemy with bayonets. Bayonets in World War II? Droll Sergeant Sharp, I wrote, was the butt of nightly barracks charades with his "Thrust, thrust, like unto thus," a clumsy clown demonstrating the *coup de grace.*

I added in the letter a graphic memory of the unit I had just left behind, recalling the cacophony of D Company's roll call sounding across Belmont Plateau just before dawn -- Tucker, Kreskinski, Pistininzzi, Ortuno, Pagnoni, Georgoiliamos, Sperling, Holland, Constein .... "All present and accounted for." It seemed longer ago than two weeks.

The weeks rolled on in Goldsboro until our batallion finally reached the magic Week Thirteen. Hanging around the day room, I counted the hours until my leave would begin. A major SNAFU struck like a twister: my name appeared on orders to proceed to the University of Toledo CTD -- without leave! I stormed off to the PX and called Amy.

Still smarting, I boarded a troop train for Toledo. The Air Corp's recruiting had been too successful: pre-cadets were put in a holding pattern called College Training Detachments. In campuses all over the country, they were immersed in classroom instruction while they waited to move into flight training.

Toledo turned out to be my softest six weeks in the service, the only real break I was to get. Here on the campus of a perennial basketball power, we were housed in a large field house. The facilities were great and the food so rich I broke out in acne. Discipline was firm, starting with roll call on the football field at 0500.

I can hear these two Southern characters yelling out their corny bromide at reveille every morning, "Fall out with collar stays and jock straps."

The people of the city seemed glad to have us, setting up dances on Saturday nights, inviting us to church then to their homes for Sunday dinner. I was lucky in a special way. Having already received my bachelor's degree, I had to take only one course, physics, an hour a day. The rest of the time I played tennis on the university's clay courts, often with the city woman's champion. What a deal.

After a quick six weeks, our group boarded a troop train for San Antonio Aviation Cadet Center, SAACC. My eyes popped wide as buttons when I got my first glimpse of the gigantic base, even wider the next day when I took in the whole squadron of cadets in their weekly parade of wooden soldiers.

Our main business at SAACC was Evaluation and Classification. Every other day we were on work detail, usually KP. My job, from morning to night, was peeling a mountain of spuds. Sounds terrible, but as I had before in the 722nd, I found it the best detail a GI could pull in the kitchen.

I remember the classification tests -- depth perception rods, manual dexterity, record player disk, the rod and hole, and others. In the hearing test I was surprised to learn I'm deaf to certain frequencies. Apparently that's normal; it didn't disqualify me.

I got open post twice. A few of us visited the Alamo then walked the pleasant streets of the city.

When the two weeks ended, I'd qualified for pilot, navigator, and bombardier. I chose pilot. Then the Class of 44-G (graduation August '44) moved across the road for Pre-flight, taking with them a salary increase of twenty-five bucks.

For the third time, I was going to have basic training! I actually got to enjoy the calisthenics and sharp close-order drill. But the obstacle course was something else -- a five-mile run, a creek to jump, ropes to climb, an eight-foot wall to negotiate. But I never felt better. My morale was top drawer.

I was assigned to Group W. I recall some of the fellows: Genovese from Philadelphia (he later washed out); baby-faced Steve Dunthorne from Annecortes, Washington; J.P. Foley from Boston; Stan Fram from Worcester, Massachusetts; Leonard Howell from Valdosta, Georgia; and Asa Cezaux from Humble, Texas. I remember him especially because of his name and because he was ten years older than the rest of us. The word was his family owned oil wells.

It was on the rifle range at SAACC that I came upon the military phenomenon called "Maggie's Drawers." To hit a target two hundred yards away with the 30-caliber rifle, which packed a whopping kick, I aimed a target width to the left. I missed the target completely every time and kept the crew downrange busy giving me the raspberries by waving their huge red flag, Maggie's Drawers.

Later, as an officer, I was issued a 45-caliber pistol. Fortunately, I could sign my own certificate of qualification. If I ever met an enemy, he had nothing to fear from me.

It was Christmastime. I spent a lonely day in a USO in downtown San Antonio, the highlight my call home. Amy sounded as chipper as she could; I'm afraid I didn't hold up my end.

Our group's next move was to nearby Uvalde. We said goodbye to the Alamo with strains of "Deep within my heart lies a melody..." and yodels of "Ahh, haa, San Antone."

The airfield in Uvalde was named for John Nance Garner, FDR's vice-president, whose home was there. Although completely grass, the field itself was better than

I'd expected in this desolate part of south Texas. It was a civilian flight school supervised by the Air Corps.

I was in a flight team with Pete Economos from Saco, Maine; Gus Forsman from L.A.; John Laird from Wellsville, Pa.; and G.D. Trader from Missouri.

Arriving at Garner Field, I felt more anxious than eager. Was it fear, lack of self-confidence? I knew this: the specter of washing out and being sent back to Slattery in Philadelphia, tail between my legs, haunted me daily.

On the second day, five nervous cadets sat on our chutes on the flight line anxiously awaiting our instructor, Lew Pruitt. We spotted him walking toward us, a small, unimposing man. He pointed to me. "Okay, Cadet Constein, you're first."

As we strode to the Fairchild PT-19, I wondered how I'd react. Would I get sick in the spins, the rolls, the loops I knew were coming? I crawled in and combed the front seat for the safety belt. After demonstrating the zigzag taxi procedure, Pruitt revved up the engine, and the slim beauty rolled down the grass strip as though she had all the time in the world to lift off. I struggled to focus, fighting off a vivid image, inexplicably, of Milton's Satan on his solitary flight to the Gates of Hell.

My hand lightly on the stick and feet on the rudder pedals, I was a mere passenger. We climbed to 3000 feet. Suddenly Pruitt put the plane into a tight roll, and gravity pulled on my face and stomach. Then came a spin down to 500 feet. I felt queasy. Speaking through the gosport, he told me to let him know when I'd had enough. We climbed again. After a dozen loops, snap rolls, and slow rolls, I began feeling green and told him I wanted to land. He misunderstood.

"More?" he said. "Okay, we'll do more." We flew to the perimeter of the training area. Looking down, I saw the town of Uvalde. I thought of Fleetwood -- neat grid of streets, pretty houses, green lawns and colorful gardens. Pruitt gave me five more long minutes of dizzying maneuvers, and we returned to the field and landed. My head light, my stomach churning, I jumped to the ground, wobbly as an infant on his first steps.

After five hours of instruction, I was ready to solo. "Remember," Pruitt said, "keep watching for a field to land in in case of an emergency." I recited the checklist to myself, not once but twice. I pushed the throttle, and the prop became a silver disk. Like a miracle, the butterflies in the slipstream of my mind vanished.

I wrote to Amy and described my bravado solo flight -- daring loops and aerobatics, bold forays into dark, cumulus castles, peaceful shuttles in and out of cotton balls, then a smooth, silky landing. I told her how unimaginably beautiful the earth looked from a plane, and how peaceful it was up there.

That was my solo; I was committed. My impression of flying was what I had expected: the thrill was not in speed, not in aerobatics, but in the unspeakable beauty of the earth viewed from my cockpit.

Carl F. Constein

The Dreaded E Ride

A BT-13 had flown into Garner Field at Uvalde one day, the biggest single-engine plane we'd ever seen up close, a giant compared to the PT-19. Aware that it was our next trainer, we swarmed over it like insects.

A few weeks later, our class of 44-G completed Primary with only two washouts. We were bused north to Waco for Basic flight training, Waco Number 1 it was called. Cadet officers were assigned to greet us. Dripping with arrogance, they treated us like plebes.

The next morning we met our instructors, Air Corps officers, not civilians. Unlike the cadet officers, they seemed like nice guys, easy-going and relaxed. I figured I'd like Basic, even though the 450 horsepower B-13 had three times more power than the PT-19 and scared me a bit.

The officers themselves were impressive, but Waco Number 1 was not well managed; there were too many changes of instructors. I had three in four weeks, the last one a Lieutenant Huckaby, notorious for putting cadets up for E rides -- not E for Excellence this time, but E for Elimination. He was a cocky, good-looking Texan who made no secret of "wanting to get out of this baby-sitting outfit" and get into combat overseas. Earlier he'd put up two of my buddies, Foley and Grant, for E rides and, sadly, both washed out.

Huckaby's sour, brusque manner reminded me of Sergeant Nuckles back in Belmont Plateau. With Huckaby in the back seat, I was sweaty and shaky. I did a lousy job one day, and of course he wrote me up for an E ride. Okay, if I washed out, I rationalized, I'd simply become a navigator. Fortunately, I had only a day to wait for the check ride. My nonchalant attitude may have helped. After the check pilot and I landed, I swaggered back to the barracks, my best smile show g that the matter was never in doubt.

The only other bad memory from Basic was shooting night landings on a bumpy landing strip marked off by smudge pots on an outlying field. Somehow we survived.

So much for Basic. At the end of May, half of us crossed the road to Blackland Field for the final leg, multi-engine training, the other half left Waco for single engine Advanced. I never learned how the Air Corps made those decisions. For me it was certainly the right one: multi-engine bombers or transports rather than single-engine fighters. Our plane in Advanced was the Cessna twin-engine AT-17, the "Bamboo Bomber."

Once we got to this final stage of our training, it was a sure bet we'd make it all the way -- unless we did something really stupid, like losing our way on a night flight (the blue street lights of Austin were a big help), failing an instrument check, cracking up, or, apparently most serious of all, scraping a wing tip while taxiing. Later overseas I learned what a grave offense the Air Corps considered that.

Advanced was a happy time. Except for a few cadets who'd become flight officers because they goofed up, we'd soon be second lieutenants. We were fitted for uniforms. I thought of how big a thing the military uniform had been when I was stuck at home and could only envy my officer friends I saw walking the streets of Fleetwood.

But a cadet could never take for granted he'd make it. On the last day of our training, sadly, two cadets of our squadron had their AT-11's tail chewed off by a plane behind them in the landing pattern. They crashed, two cadets and the instructor killed.

Amy and I were planning to be married four days after I got my wings. A leave by no means a certainty, I warned her not to make plans for a fancy wedding.

August 4, 1944 -- graduation day! After breakfast I milled about the assembly room with my exuberant buddies, back-slapping, joshing, aware we might never see each other again. The CO burst in, accompanied by a sergeant lugging a carton of wings and commissions. As I walked up to receive mine, I thought of Amy. How I wished she were there to share the moment.

The raucous celebration died down to a diminuendo as spanking-new officers pinned on their wings and bars and awaited act two -- orders to report for transitional training. The word around Blackland was that the worst assignment to pull was Reno, training base for the Hump.

A captain came in and called out our names. My hands shook as I read the mimeographed orders -- "Report to 565th AAF Base Unit, Reno Army Air Base." My heart sank. Quickly I skipped ahead, searching for a favorite military phrase. There they were, the magical words -- "ten days delay en route."

I called Amy and took a bus to the train station. My first time sleeping in a Pullman car, I arrived in Harrisburg early Monday morning, too early, I feared, for Amy and Uncle

Carl to be there. As I hurried off the platform and into the station, I spotted them. I ran up, ignored Uncle Carl for the moment, and gave Amy a big hug and kiss.

"Thank Goodness they gave you a leave," Amy said. "The wedding's all set, Dear."

In spite of my warning, Amy had made plans for a big church wedding. Really, it was her Aunt Gertrude who provided the elaborate wedding. St. Mark's Reformed Church was festooned with flowers. But if you're going to have a military wedding, you need a military best man.

Fate doesn't take a holiday when there's a war on. Dick Mellinger, the friend who'd tried to talk me into cadets in the first place, was also home on leave. He was happy to be my best man. The wedding came off perfectly, and after a modest reception in Amy's house (her mother insisted on that rather than accepting Aunt Gertrude's offer of a country club reception), we left for Philadelphia in Uncle Carl's Pontiac. Philadelphia? Poetic justice, would you say, after my bad experience with the 722nd?

Our night of fulfillment was delayed a bit. As we pulled up to park, the fan belt tore and I carried buckets of water to refill the radiator. We went into the Warburton Hotel to register. They made our reservation for the wrong night! They called and got us a room in another hotel.

After a two-day honeymoon, we returned home and stayed at Amy's mother's. We were together constantly, our best moments shimmering like wine. Ten rapturous days distilled into five before our eyes ... then three ... then one.

"The happiest days of my life," Amy whispered as she saw me off with a long kiss.

I was assigned to Reno via a short, puzzling tour at Goodfellow Field, San Angelo, in western Texas. I was sent there to be a flight instructor! A flight instructor? The situation was SNAFU, to say the least. About a dozen of us had no quarters on the base. We stayed with civilians in their homes, passing by Steve's Ranch House every day on our way to the base, never stopping, too naive to know it was one of the most famous steak houses in Texas. I can't remember what I did at Goodfellow, if anything. I believe someone bungled our orders, and everyone was happy to get us the devil out of there. Next stop, Reno Army Air Force Base.

If there's one time in a man's military service that his pride overwhelms him, I suspect it's immediately after he gets his commission. I had heard in Waco that officers could live off-base in Reno. Without checking it out, I told Amy to take a train to Reno. She'd graduated from Kutztown State Teachers College in May and, anticipating this sort of thing, took a job in a dress shop rather than applying for a teaching position.

I met her at the train station. Sitting for three days and nights on a day coach, covered in soot, she looked more like a waif than a bride. When she asked where we were going to live, I had to confess that wasn't yet settled.

Enter Chuck Bodors. He and his wife were also looking for a place to stay. It took some luck and scrambling, but the four of us found a brand-new, not-yet-lived-in low-income housing unit for rent. It was furnished sparsely, but it was clean. What a break.

Not completely. Bonnie Bodor was obnoxious and aggressive in her affected Southern charm. She was the opposite of Amy, who could handle herself in her own sincere way, but was no match for an overbearing shrew. The four of us shared the two-bedroom apartment. The cooking, the decisions, the differences -- it was too much for Amy, especially during the day when I was away on the base. Like me, Amy had never been away from home. Between that pressure and the realization that I'd soon be going overseas, our marriage got off to a rocky start.

I was assigned to Flight A of the class of C-9-B. It took me a week to get used to sitting in an airplane twenty feet off the ground. The C-46 was the Air Corps' big cargo bird, wings of an eagle, powerful enough to fly over the Himalayas' high peaks with ease. I scanned the Sierra Nevadas, mere hillocks, I suspected, beside the mighty mountains I'd soon face.

After six weeks I was ordered to Nashville on a ten-day delay en route. We took a Pullman car home. My leave was happy but bittersweet. A long separation was imminent. After the leave, Uncle Carl and Aunt Peg drove us to Harrisburg, where I boarded a train for Nashville, a staging area for overseas.

I don't remember anything about Nashville, but I vividly recall the next stop -- Miami Beach. What they said about it was true -- balmy, gentle breezes, sun-blanched beaches. A "moon over Miami" flooded my room in the Floridian Hotel. I lay on the bed and meditated.

"It's a Long, Long Way...."

It's a long, long way to Mohanbari, even farther than to Tipperary. Ensconced as I was in the Floridian Hotel on the beach of Miami Beach, there was no place in my psyche for war, for the Hump. If the Air Corps was going to lose me, as they did in San Angelo, why couldn't it have been here?

My name on the Ferrying Command's manifest, I was indeed accounted for. On October 25 I boarded a Pan Am C-54 for the Crescent run to India. Secure in my B-4 bag was a special gift from Amy, a small, leather-bound book of Psalms which I loved so much, a talisman against fear and danger.

About two and a half hours out I sensed we were on a slow descent. No way could we be close to our first stop, the Azore Islands. What's going on? everyone asked. We were going in at Bermuda. I looked down at the vivid blue-green waters of the Atlantic. As we got closer, I spotted battleships and destroyers on all sides of the gleaming island. How could these little toys patrol the high seas? What a beautiful sight!

We'd landed to correct an engine problem. After two hours, we were off again. At least I'd seen lovely Bermuda.

The flight was as smooth as a glider tow, the seat was comfortable, and I was soon asleep. Even deadheading, I was developing a pilot's sixth sense of something different, a change in altitude, perhaps the plane's attitude, the sound of the engines, the pitch of the props. Feeling a descent, I woke up in the middle of the night and watched the pilot bring the DC-4 in on a tiny landing strip smack in the middle of the ocean. We'd reached the Azores, those bleak volcanic islands which control the Western shipping lanes.

I was groggy when I stepped off the plane. It was pitch black; I saw absolutely nothing. We had a bite to eat, mystery food, and after we were refueled, we took off for Casablanca.

Ah, Humphrey Bogart and Ingrid Bergman. "Here's looking at you, kid." But that came later. Casablanca, white houses? Yes. But exotic? Try filthy, overcrowded, repulsive, impoverished, stinky. I can still hear the croaking horn of the dilapidated bus as we sped through crowded streets. "Out our way, I'm driving Americans," the proud driver was signalling his fellow wogs.

The barracks were quaint but disgustingly dirty, the stench overpowering, my introduction to the ways and culture of the peoples of the East. The-hole-in-the-ground toilet was just the first of a string of culture shocks.

The service is full of guys who can't resist a joke. A pilot I hadn't met before decided to have some fun with a wog assigned to take care of the area. The guy hid his pistol under his pillow, pretending it had been stolen. The wog went wild, moaning, folding his hands and looking heavenward, screaming in a gibberish of French mixed with his native tongue. I approached him with my college French and caught enough to learn he'd be fired if the pistol had indeed been snitched. The lieutenant continued the ruse for another fifteen minutes. Then he reached under the pillow, pulled the pistol out, and held it high. The lackey's face lit up in a smile so wide it strained his cheeks, and he uttered a piece of GI slang which traveled the world -- "Huba, Huba."

We boarded a C-46 for Tripoli. It was fitted out with two rows of bucket seats running the length of the plane, passengers facing each other across the cabin. For parachutists for whom the Curtiss Commando was designed, this arrangement was ideal. But for passengers it was awkward and uncomfortable.

Let me confess here that I always felt uneasy in the C-46, whether as pilot or passenger. It became my plane; why would I feel that way? I never felt uneasy about the planes I flew in training. What did I know about the C-46 that made me fear it?

Until I got to the Hump, nothing. My alarm was unreasonable, really, an intuitive feeling, perhaps, that a plane this size (108 foot wingspan) was just too big to be powered by only two engines. When I began flying the Hump, I soon learned the C-46 did in fact have serious problems -- engine failures, de-icer wing boots easily damaged and usually removed, ineffective carburetor heaters, hydraulic fluid leaks, runaway props, explosions. The plane had been pressed into service before it was thoroughly flight-tested, and six months after the first thirty arrived in Assam for duty on the Hump, more than seven hundred modifications were ordered.

Pilots of the 433rd Troop Carrier Group in Australia knew nothing about the C-46's flaws when it replaced their C-47s. Shortly after the pilots were checked out in the new plane, (one takeoff and one landing) Dick Hart, a friend of mine from home, ferried a plane-load of air crews from Sidney to Brisbane. Curious about the plane, one pilot wandered into the cockpit. He asked Dick how much time he had in the C-46.

Dick looked at his watch and answered, accurately, "Oh, about a half-hour."

Dick said the guy turned white and hurried back to the cabin, not knowing whether to believe him or not.

Still, the C-46 seemed as safe and meek as a trainer compared to another Hump nightmare, the C-109. Converted from the reliable 4-engine B-24 Liberator bomber, it was a flying gas tank, its cargo hold fitted out with several non-metal tanks. Once they were airborne, it was reported, none crashed in Hump service. But if the colossus failed to lift off? An inferno! The other B-24 Liberator variant, the cargo-carrying C-87, had a good record on the Hump.

Tripoli was a gas stop. We saw bullet-riddled hanger doors, evidence of the fierce Rommel-Montgomery battles, chess games in the desert.

We boarded again and headed to Cairo, flying over Bengasi. If I knew nothing about Casablanca or Tripoli, I certainly knew about the famous capital of Egypt. I gasped. There they were -- the pyramids, one of the seven wonders of the ancient world, brilliantly lit by a full moon. Is this real? Is this me, a country boy from Fleetwood?

Payne Field had a surprisingly modern, stateside air terminal. I recall talking with two Chinese diplomats en route home after a visit to Washington. Dave Zimmerman, my history teacher, would have loved that, always eager to test his belief that Chiang Kai Chek's Kuomintang was more intent on holding off the Chinese communists than in fighting the Japs.

Our billet was at the edge of the city. After we settled in, four of us took a cab to see the sights. It was dusk. We spotted a caravan of seven tethered camels lumbering Indian file, carrying their heavy cargo into the city. The rider of the lead camel was sound asleep. Our Casablanca joker had more up his sleeve.

"Stop the cab," he yelled. He got out, led the lead camel to the other side of the road and headed the scroungy column back out of town. A good laugh for us, but a major misfortune for one unlucky camel driver.

Our flight was on high priority; we stayed only one night at each stop. One night was too long at our next stop, Abadan, Iran (Persia until six years earlier). It was the hottest, most miserable place I've ever visited. Here on the edge of the desert, a simoom wind blew sand incessantly, even covering our food as we ate. I recall seeing Russian pilots flying our P-39s there. Later I saw, standing out in high relief in contrast to the desolate surroundings, a stunning, beautifully-dressed Eurasian girl on the arm of an English officer. I thought of Amy.

We boarded the next morning for our final leg, Karachi-- in western India then, capital of Pakistan now. It was completely cloudless and dry during my three-week stay. We stayed in a huge encampment built by the British when it appeared they might retreat from North Africa.

In the barracks we met a group of Hump pilots who had completed their tours and were headed home. A few were hot dogs, but most appeared sobered by their experiences. I learned about the weather -- the strong prevailing westerly winds, the downdrafts, the monsoon, the severe turbulence inside cumulonimbus thunderheads too high to fly over, the ice on the wings and in the carburetors. Jap planes? I asked. Not any more, they assured me.

It was scary to hear about the frequent engine failures and about the slim chances of surviving if you bailed out. But there was one piece of good news: after six hundred fifty hours over the Hump, a pilot was finished and would be rotated home. Most of the returning pilots had been in India only seven months.

Our orders were secret and our travel top priority. The Crescent run had delivered us to Karachi in good time. Why were we languishing in this hot, miserable hellhole for three weeks? Finally a C-46-load of us left for Assam, the eastern-most province of India. It was the end of October, the end of the monsoon.

On the flight across the subcontinent of India, land of ancient mystery, I looked down at brown fields, barren or fallow. Later, when I took a jeep to the village of Dibragarh, I got the feeling the natives couldn't afford to buy seed. What a waste.

About three hours into the flight, the copilot came back to the cabin to tell us we were in for a treat: the famed Taj Mahal was dead ahead. In a few minutes I caught a glimpse of that amazing monument, its majestic dome and four stately minarets sparkling in the sun. Coleridge flashed into my mind in large bold letters:

In Xanadu did Kubla Khan
A stately pleasure dome decree,
Where Alph, the sacred river, ran
Through caverns measureless to man
Down to a sunless sea ....

In an experience as scary as any flights I had over the Hump, I later got an up-close, too close, view of the Taj.

We landed in Agra and stayed in unusually clean buildings resembling stables, white-washed, brick-floored, with cots called charpoys for beds. I slept well.

The next morning we took off for Assam province on the last leg of our long journey. The end of the line for me was not Mohanbari but Chabua (CHAB-wah), the largest of the Hump bases, flying only C-46s. All the fields had enchanting, musical names -- Sookerating, Jorhat, Dinjan, Tingmari, Tezpur, Warazup, Dergoan, Mohanbari, Tezgaon, Kharagour, Shamsherenagar.

About two hours out of Agra, I became aware of a subtle change in the scenery. The arid land was partially replaced by greenery. And as I looked ahead, the flat countryside gave way to rising mountain peaks, the famous First Ridge of the Hump. Before we approached Chabua, we flew over the broad Brahmaputra River. Overflowing after six months of monsoon rains, it looked more like a huge lake than a moving stream. I thought of my Schuylkill River back in Reading, a mere creek.

Chabua, finally! I stepped off the C-46 and looked around at the airfield -- desolate, dusty, umber, as barren as a desert. The control tower and shacks on the flight line looked spent and breathless, the set for an old western. I was incredulous later when I realized that the whole Hump operation and all its airfields had to be less than three years old, the China-Burma-India (CBI) theater itself not much older.

In spite of its decrepit appearance, the field was buzzing with activity, planes taking off and landing every couple minutes. I soon discovered that Chabua was the O'Hare Field of India.

A Jeep drove up. "Get in, Lieutenant," a sergeant said. Sneering, he added, "I'll take you to the George Washington Hotel."

The bamboo basha, built without nails, looked inviting -- British colonial, thatchroofed, surrounded on three sides by a lush plantation of tea prized the world over. Clear in my mind is a rich painting -- young Hindu girls, their babies on their backs, picking the tender tea leaves.

"Find yourself a bed," the sergeant said and drove away. I had no delusions about a second lieutenant's perks, but scrounging around for your own bed? I claimed one in a corner and unpacked my bag, loading its contents into the only furniture, a beat-up foot locker like the deadman's chest of legend. The wall was plastered with pin-ups of Betty Grable, Rita Hayworth, Dinah Shore, Ginger Rogers, and a bevy of other shapely beauties. I learned later why the bed was available: three pilots who'd slept in it were killed, two in crashes, one bailed out over the Hump and never returned. Leave it to the military to label everything. I was in Barracks 5, Bay 3, Bed 3L.

If I expected an orientation the next day, I was quickly put right. I asked other "guests" in the "hotel" where to locate things on the base. "Just roam around, you'll find them." Giving back the kind of gracious reception they had had, no doubt.

That night, after the first of what would be countless Spam dinners, a corporal drove up to the basha and called out, "Lieutenant Constein, Lieutenant Constein."

I walked out to the porch. "Here," I said.

"Report to flight operations at 2200 hours. After this, check the bulletin board." He left me standing like a stump. Welcome to the friendly 1333rd AAF Base unit!

Here I was, twelve thousand miles from home in a God-forsaken place nobody ever heard of. My thoughts were all inward. It wasn't until I got home and thought about it that I realized how close I'd been to places famous in adventure and modern history. Directly west of Chabua, a two-hour flight away, were Mt. Everest and a place that in its name alone conjures up dreams of earthly beauty and mystery -- Kashmir. The eastern terminal of the Hump was Kunming, China. To the southeast, two hours away by air, lay that country that still evokes bitter memories and anguish for America -- Vietnam.

I had less than three hours to get myself set for my first flight on the fabled Hump. It was getting dark, and the rain which had been steady all day became a downpour as a fierce storm struck. Bright lightning lit up the basha. I couldn't sit still. I felt queasy. It was a long wait.

Flight to Nowhere

Just before 2200, nervous as a cat, I walked into Operations. It was raining, hard. Captain Owens was filing a flight plan. "Let's go for coffee," he said when he finished. We walked next door to the tiny room beneath the tower. Streaks of lightning split the night sky, followed by peals of thunder booming like tribal drums.

So late at night, I was surprised to see all the activity on the flight line and in operations. Somehow I thought our flight might be the only one scheduled.

"We're not going to take off in this crap?" I said.

"Hell, this isn't bad."

I made a face.

"It's my last trip. We'll make it a good one."

After we finished our coffee, we walked outside, threw our chutes on the spare seat and got into the waiting jeep. The driver crawled down the flight line, hail pelting the canvas top, sheets of rain blowing in through the cracks. We came to 0798, its numbers barely discernible. She looked like a derelict, alone and forlorn in her revetment at the end of the line. We grabbed our chutes, climbed the ladder to the cargo hold, and walked through to the cockpit, greeting the radio operator, already at work at his station just behind the cockpit. I put my chute on the right seat, sat down, and fastened the seat belt. The survival kit in the chute made the seat lumpy. Following Owens' lead, I didn't fasten the leg or shoulder straps of the chute.

I pulled out the checklist. After Owens nodded, I called out: "Fuel tanks full, mixture control rich, hydraulic fluid checked, controls free...."

"Ready to go," Owens said. "Call the tower."

Timidly, I made my first call. "Victor George, request permission to taxi." As we taxied to the end of the runway, my heart raced. My hands felt like wet sponges. I shook my head. God, I never thought I'd take off in weather like this. Owens ran up the right engine, checked the mag drop, then repeated the check on the left engine.

"Call the tower," he ordered.

"Victor George, Zero Seven Nine Eight ready for takeoff. Over."

"Zero Seven Nine Eight. You're cleared for takeoff."

A crosswind tugged hard on the big bird as she lumbered down the runway, a behemoth bulging with a volatile load of -- not oil for the lamps of China, but gasoline in 55-gallon drums for its armies. Let's go, let's go! My adrenalin shot up when I saw the end of the runway coming up fast. Up! Up! my mind cried. With only fifty feet to spare, we reached 85mph and lifted off. Within seconds, we were in pea soup, flying on instruments. As we climbed, we were tossed about like a toy -- a deluge of water, a howling snowstorm, ice driving hard against the windshield and already forming on the wings. At 6000 feet severe turbulence became our master, air speed dropping to near stalling at 80 mph then rushing past a redlined 280mph as we dove like a roller coaster. I stared at the instrument panel, seeing nothing. My eyes grew wide as half-dollars when I heard hail crashing against the fuselage like a summons of doom.

We were on a heading of 210 degrees, the radio compass set on the Moran frequency. The needle fluctuated wildly on either side of its expected position. I'd received no orientation on the route, but on my own I'd determined there were no high peaks until we headed east on what was officially called the "Easy" route. When we reached 7000 feet, the compass needle swung 180 degrees.

"It's a local storm. We'll be out of it soon." Owen's calm reassured me.

We climbed to 10,000 feet, took a heading of 123 degrees, still climbing. The Naga Hills, the First Ridge of the Hump, lay just ahead.

"Put on your oxygen mask," Owens directed.

Five minutes later I looked ahead and saw a magnificent sight -- bright stars! We were at 12,000 feet. Just as I started to relax, the left engine backfired several times like Jake Boyer's old Ford truck on the streets of Fleetwood. Holy Hell, I said, half to myself. My heart raced. Owens put carburetor heat on both engines and motioned for me to hold the levers. He moved the left mixture control to automatic rich. The engine spit and hissed, and coughed like a consumptive. I was sure it was going to quit. It wasn't fair, my heart told me -- Owens on his last flight, me on my first.

The engine continued cutting out, the whole plane shaking like my Black Widow when I started it on cold mornings. Sweat broke out on my forehead. Owens turned to 270 degrees. Oh no! We were going back into the storm!

Owens motioned for the radio operator. "Tell Victor George we're coming back. No Mayday yet." He said to me, "Set the compass to the Chabua beacon."

My mind flashed to Amy and Mother.

The engine knocked so hard I was afraid it'd break off. "I'm going to have to feather this bastard. I want you to help trim the ship." Suddenly, as though saying that brought good luck, the engine settled down. I exhaled loudly. Back in the heart of the storm, the hail and snow and wind even more violent, the little airplane on the artificial horizon on the instrument panel came close to tipping off. If that happened, we wouldn't have any idea whether we were upside down or right side up.

"Tell Victor George we're about fifteen minutes out."

"Roger, Zero Seven Nine Eight," the tower replied. "Traffic's heavy. Hold at 5000 feet. Call when you cross the station."

The engine continued to run smoothly. Lightning lit the sky; hail and snow were everywhere. I said a prayer for the engine to hold and the turbulence to let up.

When we crossed the beacon, I called the tower.

"Roger, Zero Seven Nine Eight. Descend to 4500 feet. Altimeter 27.98. Over."

"Roger, wilco."

Owens turned to a heading of 50 degrees, flew for one minute, did a standard rate turn and took the reciprocal heading of 230 degrees. He maintained the holding pattern, all the time waiting for clearance to descend, 500 feet at a time, until the planes below us had landed and we were number one to land.

We broke out of the weather on the final approach, about 200 feet off the ground, and landed without incident. I expelled my breath in a loud gush and sank down in the seat. After the "Follow Me" truck guided us to a revetment, a jeep took us to operations for debriefing. I entered into my log: "Chabua to Chabua." It had been a flight to nowhere. Flight time -- one hour.

The driver jeeped us through the mud to the dispensary for our medicinal two shots of Old Crow. "Good luck on your next last trip, Captain," I said. "I hope it'll be better than this one." I raised my shot glass in a toast.

"Thanks. And the same to you."

I staggered back to basha 5, fastened the mosquito bar of bed L3, and crawled in. Within minutes I was dead to the world.

"I Will Lift Up Mine Eyes...."

The next morning I awoke to music. Where am I? I saw the mosquito netting and knew. Yet the American pop music? I got dressed and ambled outside, following the melody wafting in from somewhere beyond our bay.

The sun was bright, the first time I'd seen Ol Sol since I arrived in Chabua three days ago. Hearing voices, I walked to the tea plantation near our basha and watched young girls, cackling ceaselessly, most with babies strapped to their backs, as they plucked the tender tea leaves.

"Tumble Weed" was coming from the two-bed bay next door. I stepped back into my basha and inquired about our neighbors. No one seemed to know who they were and why they merited special privileges. They played the same record on their victrola over and over again, driving some of the old-timers nuts. Later I heard the reverse side, "Pretty Blue Eyes," prophetic for me perhaps, for after the war our daughter Anne was born with the prettiest blue eyes you ever saw.

I lay on my bed and took stock. What a wild ride last night, that first ride. In the states, if a pilot had a close call, the Air Corps got him into the air immediately. Did anyone even report our close call? There'd be no mollycoddling here.

After a shower and a shave, I walked to the mess hall for breakfast then strolled to base operations to learn what I could. A sergeant gave me a map and a handful of charts showing airfields and elevations, runway directions, course bearings, and radio frequencies. Back in the basha, I cut the charts and pasted them into my pocket notebook. I added my own notes: check points en route, auxiliary fields for emergency landings, and landing and takeoff patterns. It became my bible, as essential as my parachute.

It became my log book as well. I recorded destinations, flight times, and running tot   icipating six hundred fifty hours, my ticket to going home. I'm surprised now, and more than a little disappointed in myself, at how disorganized and messy my little book is. But it proved a useful, at times vital, companion on many flights. I cherish it and treat it with care, its pages faded but legible.

I soon learned how little there was to do on the base -- no PX, no theater or rec center, no ping pong or pool table. But there was an officers club, its walls resplendent with luscious nudes to keep us company. I went to the club occasionally; it was lively only on Saturday nights.

We were all at the club at times for something decidedly not recreational -- pilot briefings about technical problems, especially the nagging dilemma of how to handle the ever-present ice in the carburetor. Herb Fisher, Curtiss-Wright tech rep/test pilot on the scene, advised us to apply heat whenever we suspected ice, then throw the mixture control to idle rich or full rich if more correction was needed. Some pilots vehemently disagreed, arguing it was better to wait until they got an indication of ice before applying heat. It seemed academic and overdone. The bar was closed during those charming sessions, but at least we had the murals to detract us.

I have a bad, bad memory of one Saturday night at the club. I didn't drink much before I got into the service -- too poor, too wet behind the ears. I was drinking whiskey that night. It wasn't top shelf, but it was okay. When the bar ran out of whiskey, I switched to gin, Dixie Belle gin. The party went on into the night.

The next morning I was so sick it hurt to walk. I stayed in bed all day. I thought I'd die. Luckily, I wasn't scheduled to fly. I rationalized my misconduct away: it wasn't my fault the club ran out of whiskey. I haven't touched a drop of gin since.

In the basha I read a lot, played bridge, and, occasionally, chess with a cocky flight officer. Our competition ended abruptly when he cracked up at Kunming, killing himself and dozens of Chinks in a village beyond the landing strip. He came in too high that day. He should not have tried to go around, especially loaded, especially in the high elevation of Kunming. In the most important game of his life, my chess buddy made the wrong move.

Amy had sent me the books I requested, and more -- including books of poetry, Emerson's Essays, some modern novels, and the King James Bible. In my childhood years in Sunday School, I never got the point of many of the stories. In Chabua, I took another look, going beyond the stories to the exquisite Book of Psalms Amy gave me when I left home, becoming familiar with the lyrical books which remain my favorites -- Job, Ecclesiastes, Proverbs, Song of Solomon, and, especially, John's mystical Revelation.

I found out I'd be flying every other day or so. The procedure was to check the bulletin board and get yourself to operations on time. If I was slated for a late night flight, the Charge of Quarters, I was told, would come to my bed and call me. Later, on such nights, I slept fitfully, waiting for an eerie beam of light and a spook to shake me and whisper my name.

I exhaled loudly when I saw my second flight would be in the daytime, to Kunming, takeoff at 0800. I hit the sack early.

I awoke the next morning to a bright, sunny day, thank goodness. Looking east over the First Ridge, I saw giant cumulus rising to over 30,000 feet. I walked into operations. The pilot introduced himself. He looked young. I was surprised when he told me he'd had forty-nine trips under his belt. I remember his face but not his name. Unfortunately, except for Captain Owens and one other fellow, I didn't record the names of the crews I flew with.

Delivered to our plane, Number 608, we walked around it for the pre-flight check. It looked newer than most, fewer dents in the fuselage from hail and propeller ice. Second in line, we took off and headed south to the Moran beacon, climbing 300 feet per minute at an air speed of 145mph. In a short time we flew into a covey of pure-white, puffy cumulus, fortunately not cumulonimbus like the mess I was in two nights earlier. When the needle swung 180 degrees, we held over Moran, climbing till we reached 10,000 feet. Still climbing, we turned east and headed for China, still in the weather.

Just after we crossed the First Ridge, the Patkai Range, we broke into the clear over Burma. I gasped. Suddenly, marvelously, overhead in the cloudless sky was the sun, a white-hot furnace spewing dazzling brilliance over the jagged peaks in the distance. Sheer, absolute beauty -- gray cliffs, some variegated in black, most topped by snow-capped peaks. A favorite Psalm flashed into my mind: "I will lift up mine eyes unto the hills from whence cometh my help..." On tours to Europe and Africa since then, I've flown over marvelous sites and panoramas, but nothing compares to the Himalayas. I will never forget that first view of the Hump.

Still climbing, oxygen masks on our faces now, we flew over the thick, lush jungle of the Hukawng Valley, the richest, deepest green you'll ever see. We crossed the meandering Irrawaddy River then the Kumon Mountains, the Myitkyina (MISH-in-awe) beacon off our right wing tip. We got to our cruising altitude of 18,500 and put Dumbo on auto pilot. The air speed read 160mph, tachometer 2000 rpm. After flying over another valley and the 16,000-foot peaks separating Burma and China, I looked down on the fantastic Salween River gorge. I glanced at the altimeter and was shocked to see we were rising -- even though the nose was level and the air speed constant.

I nudged the pilot. Holding his mask away from his face, he said, "Yeah, the west wind is giving us a ridge lift. After we cross to the lee side, we'll come back down without lifting a finger."

My mind flashed to Pruitt, my Primary flight instructor. "Always know where you can put down in an emergency." I shuddered. The only place to land on this section of the Hump, the real "Rock Pile", was Yunnanyi 130 miles west of Kunming. Unless you were close, your procedure was simple: bail out and pray. Face it, I told myself, quick death over the mountains or slower death in the unknown horrors of the Burma jungle.

An apocryphal story heard around the Hump concerned a radio operator who bailed out over the jungle and became entangled in a tree. He couldn't reach his knife. His only chance to free himself was to shoot his harness off. He failed. Soon leeches and insects swarmed over his face and hands and legs. He put his last bullet into his head. I figured my trench knife was at least as important as my Colt 45; I kept it inside my holster.

We crossed the Salween gorge, then the Mekong gorge, passed over Paoshan and came to the Santsung Mountains, the highest and grandest peaks en route, the backbone of the Hump. Two hundred miles to the north was a land of mystery where the proud Himalayas rose to 23,000 feet. As we flew on, ever eastward, the terrain became less fearsome. We crossed over Tsuyung and had only eighty miles to fly to Kunming and its large, picturesque Lake Tali, a silver dollar newly minted. We flew on and landed. Kunming was the main field on the China side, accepting a plane from India or sending one home every minute or so.

The names of cities on this end of the Hump were not pleasant and melodic but harsh and guttural -- Kunming, Chanyi, Yankai, Chengkung, Tsuyung, Luliang, Yunnanyi. The only one I liked, perhaps because of fond memories of the field's gentle breeze and picturesque setting, is Paoshan. (PAY-o-shan.) Every gentle breeze now is a Paoshan breeze.

We taxied, parked, and walked to the operations building. My first visit to China. "You'll like the food here," the pilot said.

I feigned gagging.

"No, I mean it. You'll see."

After we checked in, we walked to the chow line at the other end of the building. The aroma was enticing -- eggs and bread. Fresh eggs! As we went through the line, the smiling Chink asked each of us, "Egk-es, Cho?" as though there were a choice. Simple as it was, it was the tastiest meal I'd had in a long while.

The weather was mild and beautiful in Kunming, with no humidity. After we ate, we sat on the flight line and relaxed. Alien-looking coolies in pale blue padded jackets chatted like magpies as they unloaded the 55-gallon drums of gasoline and clusters of 60mm shells. I remarked about how slowly they worked. "Actually," the pilot said, "these guys are faster than most."

On later flights I observed that Indian workers were more industrious. I was amazed at how strong they were in spite of their thin bodies. And they were trustworthy. In China, flight crews took turns guarding the cockpit. Parachute survival kits were favorite targets -- cigarettes to burn off leeches, machete, money, maps, first aid kit, compass.

"Do you know anything about war lords stealing the supplies we deliver?" I asked.

"I've heard that. I've also heard that much of what does get to Chiang is used against the Chinese communists, not the Japs."

We looked to the end of the strip where a thousand civilian Chinks were pounding away with hammers, making little rocks out of big ones. I spotted what looked like two hundred Chinese pulling a gigantic roller across the new section of the strip.

"These Chinks are queer," the pilot said. "They believe evil spirits follow them, so they sometimes run in front of a moving plane, hoping to kill off their demons. One guy told me he thought he hit a Chink while landing at Yunnanyi and reported to the tower. Their response was, "Roger on the Chink. Follow the jeep to the revetment."

"They also have a weird sense of humor," the pilot added. "Do you think they'd help one of their buddies who had a drum of gasoline roll on his foot? Hell no. They just howl in laughter."

Kunming and Luliang were in Yunnan Province. Sound familiar? It's where Mao Tse-tung recruited his people's republic, which after WWII renewed its civil war with Chiang's Nationalist government, winning out in 1949. The Nationalists retreated to Taiwan (formerly Formosa), the island ceded back from Japan after the war, and established the Republic of China (ROC) one hundred fifty miles offshore from the super giant called Mainland China. I am incredulous that Goliath allows David to live. If an attack comes, it will test the world's mettle like nothing since World War II. It will make NATO's strike against Yugoslavia over Kosovo look like war games.

By 1300 hours the plane was refueled and ready for flight. We gave a thumbs-up "Ding Hao" to the crew chief on the ground and taxied out. Our ETA in Chabua was 1800.

"Four hours?" I asked. "We came over in three."

"Yeah, we'll be bucking the prevailing westerly wind's 80mph going home. It looks as though we're in for something unusual, a clear flight all the way home."

We returned on Charlie course, about fifty miles north of the Easy course, at an altitude of 19,000 feet. The

Santsung peaks on this course were the highest we'd encounter; empty, India-bound planes could more readily handle the height. Our radio checkpoints were Yunnanyi, Yunglung, and Shingbwiyang.

The sky still cloudless, I spotted a C-87 approaching Yunnanyi field. Coming east, I had seen planes from the dozen Indian bases criss-crossing the Hump -- C-47s, C-46s, C-87s, C-109s, and C-54s.

We reached Shingbwiyang, eighty-eight miles to Chabua on a course of 307 degrees. We called the Chabua tower and were cleared for a Contact Flight Rule landing.

"Before we enter the traffic pattern," the pilot said, "go back and pour hydraulic fluid into the tank." Hydraulic leaks were just one more of old Dumbo's deficiencies.

We landed and checked in. I stuck the slip for two shots of combat whiskey into my pocket, saving it for R&R.

That night I wrote a long letter to Amy, ignoring the first flight, extolling the beauties I saw that day. I gave her a light-hearted description of the plush living conditions in my "hotel." But mainly, my letters, like every GI's, were filled with mush and kisses, and page after page fantasizing about a happy future.

My verbal lovemaking, I soon learned, was mild. Once a month I drew censor duty and read random letters written home by enlisted men. Wow!

After dinner I got into a bridge game then went to bed and dreamed of a big blue sky resplendent in beauty.

What's It All About?

The next day I poked around the base, learning what I could. Playbills were not handed out by ushers in this theater. I'd logged seven hours and thirty-five minutes yesterday. It was a start.

In November I had nine more flights, seven to Kunming, and two shorter flights to Myitkyina, Burma, (Burma became Myanmar in 1989) one hundred twenty miles southeast of Chabua. Myitkyina was my first look at the devastation of war, a city and base completely destroyed, first by the Japanese a year earlier, then retaken in August by General Stilwell's Twenty-second and Thirty-ninth Chinese Divisions after a bloody seventy-eight day siege. Not a single building remained standing. To walk through the ruins of the airfield and pick up spent shells was a profound new experience. Recapturing this strategic base allowed the Air Transport Command (ATC) to put C-47s and four-engine C-54s on a lower, more southerly course to China.

My November flight time was sixty-seven hours, twenty minutes. To reach my goal of six hundred fifty hours by June 1, I'd have to average a hundred hours a month. No problem. I had a more immediate goal: to log two hundred hours so I could check out as first pilot. I figured I'd paid my dues as copilot.

I agreed with most Hump pilots at Chabua that flying the C-46 was pretty much a one-pilot operation. A first pilot could readily operate the landing gear and flaps on his own. He could talk to the tower, change the mixture control, feather an engine, and operate any other controls. But in heavy turbulence, or if the left engine quit, the pilot needed the extra muscle of the copilot to control the plane, especially in landing. The hydraulic assist to the ailerons, flaps, and other controls was supplied by the left engine. Flying a C-46 without the left engine was like driving a car without power steering.

Of course a good copilot assured a degree of safety, not only in emergencies, but two heads are better than one in going through the half-dozen checklists. And if a pilot had his "head up and locked" and turned east instead of west after an Instrument Flight Rules (IFR) takeoff from fields in China, notably Kunming, the copilot could grab the controls and prevent a crash into the waiting mountain. But as first pilot, you never knew from one flight to the next who your copilot and crew would be. Fixed crews would have led to improved safety, certainly to better morale.

When I hear my pilot-friend Dick Gable talk about his B-17 crew in England, I realize what I missed. They were a unit, eating together, socializing together, living together. Team spirit like this might have soothed me in my loneliness and helped allay the fears I often felt. The base commander's staff gave fixed crews a brief, perfunctory trial but rejected the arrangement because, I suspect, they found the extra work onerous.

I was eager to check out as first pilot as a matter of pride, not immediate promotion in rank. And also, I considered some of the first pilots I flew with to be, shall I say, questionable. I met all kinds -- some poorly organized, some hot dogs, some unfriendly, some weirdos. I recall one who really upset me.

I walked into operations and introduced myself to the pilot. He didn't say a word and barely looked up from the flight plan he was filing. Without talking, we entered the plane and waited for clearance to taxi. He pulled a paperback out of his jacket pocket and started to read, continuing even while he taxied.

We were third in line for takeoff and moved up in order. He continued to smoke and read as I watched the plane ahead of us on its takeoff run. Something was wrong; he wasn't getting off the runway where he should. He finally lifted off, but I didn't see him climb. We heard a loud boom and saw a cloud of black smoke rise beyond the runway, the worst-case crash. In the face of almost certain death, perhaps of a friend, my pilot looked up briefly then quickly resumed reading, waiting calmly for clearance to take off.

The moment of takeoff, not landing, was the moment I feared, the crucial moment of every flight in a C-46, so prone to engine failure. I landed single engine a few times and it's no picnic, but you have power, you have altitude, you have control. If there's an unobstructed runway down there and your visibility is at least minimum, you're going to make it.

Taking off without sufficient power is something else again. Your 48,000-pound monster is bouncing down the runway, struggling to lift off at 85mph. If an engine quits now, you've had it. But if your air speed has reached 125mph when the event occurs, you might be able to maintain altitude and come in for a landing. That's the theory.

But on half my takeoffs, I was into weather, on instruments, within a minute after I left the ground. Even if I could feather the engine and maintain altitude, how did I land in a ground fog or low ceiling? Just past the runway in Chabua are several ugly scars, memorials to pilots who crashed on takeoff. I knew one of them. I wonder how many of the more than five hundred planes we lost crashed on takeoff.

I was lucky to arrive in Chabua in the fall just after the monsoon had left, taking along its inexhaustible stock of stratus and altostratus. At least I could see the ground on some flights. But there were always high cumulus clouds en route just waiting to ripen into thunderheads and ensnare you. As copilot I had plenty of time to work out checkpoints. Our best navigational guides, although weak, were the radio beacons at Shingbwiyang, Tingkawksakan, and Myitkyina in Burma. But the only completely dependable signals were at Chabua and Kunming. I also charted the exact location of the auxiliary fields of Tsuyung and Yunglung in China, and an original Flying Tigers fighter strip just north of Yunnanyi.

After the war, I learned that Paul Strunk, a teacher friend, had been with a Service of Supply unit in the Burma jungle, mainly at Shingbwiyang, for twenty-seven long months. I'd flown over him, to China and back, nearly two hundred times!

Another friend, George Spirt from Philadelphia, spent even more time, over three and a half years, as radio operator in the CBI. He told me Tokyo Rose knew all about their unit in Sylhet, Assam, one of the first to arrive in

India. The two hundred sixty specialists, all non-coms of the 98th Airdrome Squadron, filled in on detached service wherever they were needed.

Only occasionally did I see American service men other than Hump air crew and ground support. I was surprised to learn after the war that there were plenty of others around. Some were in service units, like Paul's and George's, others in fighter or bomber units. Totally in the CBI there were one hundred twenty-two commands, organizations, and units.

Looking out for myself, I learned the Hump routes like a road map. The route east, the Easy route, started with the first leg to Moran, the broad Brahmaputra with its crocodiles and hippos on the right, the First Ridge on the left. Farther on, on clear days, I spotted the Hump's forbear, the Burma Road, a giant snake sunning itself, at some places its body hacked into ugly pieces by Japanese bombers.

From the beginning, I was as fascinated as the Romantic poets had been by nature's unfailing West Wind, giving me the gift of an hour's precious time flying east, then taking back the favor and adding an hour to the return trip to India. On some days, especially in the spring and summer, a thick blanket of clouds required instrument flying from fifteen seconds after takeoff to fifteen seconds before landing. Instrument time is a badge of pride among pilots. Ironically, even though I may have seen the ground for less than an hour on a seven-hour round-trip, I could record as instrument time only the time I was actually in the soup. It was peaceful above the monsoon blanket, the sun brilliant; the only glimpses I had of Mother Earth was of a few of the highest peaks sticking out their necks.

Clear days were rare and beautiful, but scary, showing off China's highest, most treacherous peaks and Burma's forbidding jungle, home of the Savage Nagas. Like worms in fruit, monstrous thunderstorms lodged themselves in the open sky.

At night, wandering stars shining brightly above, I looked down on sheer beauty -- hundreds of Chinese villages, visible only through their blazing fires in high plains and on mountainsides, blinking fireflies greeting each other across the sky. As far as the eye could see, all was at peace.

For five of the seven hours of the round trip, the big bird soaring on auto-pilot, two giant engines humming in sync, I welcomed a swarm of miscellaneous thoughts into the cockpit -- always dreams of Amy and the happiness that awaited us, sometimes going back to my childhood, wondering how Mother was doing, and especially Father, permanently in a wheelchair. Was this really me, I mused, in this huge metal box twelve thousand miles from home?

At times I wondered what the whole Hump-CBI thing was all about; I had only a vague idea. "Ours not to reason why...." Of course I knew we were trying to hang on to China, at the time the only base for the eventual counterattack against the island of Japan. Like America, China had also been attacked by the Japs. I recalled as long ago as high school seeing Pathé News clips of Japs marching into China's Manchuria.

I had to wait until after the war to learn how and why the Hump came into being. Meeting in Ottawa two months after Pearl Harbor, President Roosevelt and Prime Minister Churchill declared their intention of supplying China through its western border, not only China itself, of course, but American units fighting with them -- the 10th Air Force, Channault's 14th Air Force, and American advisers and officers attached to Stilwell's Chinese troops. Supplies were to be transported from the port of Rangoon, Burma, north by rail to Lashio for hauling by truck to Kunming, China, over the winding seven hundred-mile Burma Road. But Rangoon fell to the Japanese.

The brass went back to the drawing boards and came up with a complex revision. Supplies from America would come into Calcutta, be shipped a thousand miles to Sadiya in India's Bramaputra Valley, be airlifted two hundred miles over the Naga Hills to Myitkyina, sent by rail and barge down the Irrawaddy River to Bhamo, then to China over the Burma Road. Engineers were rushed to Myitkyina to build a hard-surface landing strip. But the Japanese continued marching north in Burma, capturing Lashio, Bhamo, and finally Myitkyina. So much for the revised plan. The only option that remained -- fly all military supplies from India to China! The Hump!

The command had precious little to go on. Fortunately, China National Aviation Corporation, a joint venture of Chiang and Pan-American Airlines, had been flying across the Himalayas; the Air Corps could at least fly routes they'd charted.

Headquartered in Kunming, CNAC used some British and American pilots, including a few Flying Tigers who stayed on in China after Chennault's famous mercenary group had been disbanded. Going from speedy P-40s to 150mph C-47 transports must have been a culture shock. Still mercenaries, they were paid well -- three times more than we were, and they stayed in quarters three times finer. Their eastern base was Dinjan, India, a field they shared with the RAF and the U.S. Tenth Air Force, which had responsibility for the Hump.

The Tenth's first cargo-carrying flight over the Hump came on April 8, 1942 -- drums of gasoline for the planes of Jimmy Doolittle, who later that month led a morale-boosting bombing attack on Tokyo in B-25s from a carrier in the Pacific. But the Tenth, a bomb command, was not keen on flying cargo. By August, Hump tonnage was a puny seven hundred tons a month.

Chiang was extremely unhappy. There were valid explanations -- not enough planes, airfields, personnel; inadequate maintenance. Washington had to act. After an on-sight evaluation by the high command, a decision was made to put the Air Transport Command in full control of the Hump under the supervision of General Hap Arnold. The first ATC Hump flight came a few months later, on December 1, 1942.

Progress came slowly. Even the introduction in April, 1943, of the bigger C-46 with its four-ton payload did not increase tonnage significantly, primarily because it was undependable and had many engine failures and fatal accidents. Even so, after six months, ATC was delivering three thousand tons of crucial military supplies to China every month.

Not satisfied, Chiang sent his wife, a charmer if a head of state ever had one, to plead with Congress. Chennault promised that if his 14th Air Force received ten thousand tons a month, he would sink a million tons of Japanese shipping. President Roosevelt ordered Hump tonnage increased to ten thousand tons by September, a three-fold increase! Pressure was intense. General Tom Hardin ordered night flying and all-weather flying. "There will be no weather on the Hump," he declared.

As tonnage increased, so did accidents, one hundred fifty-five between June and December, 1943, resulting in one hundred sixty-eight fatalities. The word went home it was safer to fly bombing missions over Germany than to fly the Hump. Complaints from wives and parents to President Roosevelt and Congress brought results. General William H. Tunner was sent over as new CO to perform a Catch-22 miracle: increase tonnage and cut the accident rate.

A decision to supply China by air had by no means been unanimous. The British Command didn't share American enthusiasm for China's role in the war. Within the American Command, Stilwell and his supporters in the War Department, especially Marshall and Simpson, thought such aid would be too limited. They argued for a north Burma campaign and construction of the Ledo Road. But President Roosevelt, Generals Arnold and Chennault, supported by the British and Chinese, believed the road could not be completed in time to help China. The latter view proved closer to reality: eighty percent of the tonnage which reached China was airlifted.

Infighting among the leaders was fierce. Towering above all the principals was General Vinegar Joe Stilwell. Chiang, whom Stilwell dubbed "Peanut," was his chief adversary. Others on Stilwell's blacklist were Chennault and China National Aviation Corporation. Chiang ultimately came out the winner, prevailing upon President Roosevelt to dismiss Stilwell. Newcomer Tunner and General Chennault had their own ongoing feud.

The bickering and lack of clear commitment to an airlift to China was responsible for an uneven history of the

Hump. When the Hump opened in the spring of 1942, the CBI was considered a theater for holding action only. A year later, tonnage increased as the Hump supported the air offensive in China and the ground offensive in Burma. A year after that, a no-limits expansion pervaded the Hump strategy, and tonnage increased significantly. During the final months, six hundred planes landed in China every day to deliver their precious cargo.

General Tunner and I arrived in India at about the same time. I believe he liked his job better than I liked mine.

So much for the history lesson. I had a professor at Temple University who was fond of saying, "History is Twistery!"

Carl F. Constein

A Rough December

Every day my thoughts were of home. I longed to be home, to be with Amy. But I had to adjust to Chabua. Fortunately, most of the sixteen men in my bay were congenial.

But one guy in the adjoining bay, a captain, puzzled us. He'd wander into our bay at any time of day or night, drunk, a can of beer in his hand, even before breakfast. A pilot, he never flew. He was a congenial drunk, rattling on incessantly in his deep Southern drawl. Why was he still here? we wondered.

CO of the Hump, and later of the Berlin Airlift, General William H. Tunner wrote a book called *Over the Hump.* A passage in it may provide a clue to the mystery. According to Tunner, the CBI was a place to exile officers other theaters or commands didn't want. He speaks of two undesirables he knew personally, one an arrogant guy whom nobody got along with, one a drunk (higher ranking than ours) whom he "invited" to serve in India. Tunner confesses that the personnel officer of the Ferrying Division included in its India-China quota some misfits the Division didn't want, mainly command staff officers.

Tunner had been CO of the Air Corps Ferrying Division with eight thousand pilots assigned. When General George made him head of the Hump, Tunner was reluctant to leave his prestigious organization to take over a command a quarter its size. The Hump, he knew, had been a graveyard for exiled commanders, none of whom added a star to their epaulet when they left. Many Hump staff officers felt the same disdain. Tunner overcame his disappointment, worked hard, and did a superb job. But his subordinates, I believe, remained bitter about their exile and were responsible for the low morale.

The drunk in the next bay may have been one of the Ferry Command's rejects, a candidate, we all believed, for a Section Eight. That's a provision that allows personnel to receive a discharge if they are no longer fit to serve. It can also be an escape hatch for cowards clever enough to fake psychological disabilities. I know a guy from home who did.

***

One day in early December, an officer sat beside me at lunch. "Do you know a Lieutenant Constein?" I saw his insignia and recognized the base chaplain, Captain Unger.

The irony was replaced immediately by a heavier thought. It had to be Father. We ate in silence. He asked me to go with him to his office.

When he told me Father had died of pneumonia, I broke down, crying unashamedly. It was three years since he'd had that terrible stroke at work. Although I knew the answer, I asked whether I could go home on leave. I couldn't even receive a phone call.

My December log shows seven flights before December 19, with no time off for mourning. On that date I was scheduled for a flight to Kunming at 1500, an awkward time for eating and sleeping. The pilot and I met at operations and filed a flight plan. Our plane was 597.

We got to our altitude without incident. The afternoon was crystal clear. I was awed by the Himalayas' majestic beauty, capped with snow, dazzling in dappled sunlight. In capricious contrast, the Burma jungle was an endless field of broccoli. But even this beauty couldn't chase away my feeling of despair. We landed, ate our eggs, and in no time were back in the plane, headed for India.

As we climbed to altitude, an uneasy feeling settled over me. I was cold. The pilot refused to use the cockpit heater -- too risky, he said, because of fumes. I imagined I smelled an oily odor coming from the cabin. I became aware of the eerie greenish glow of the instrument panel. The mysticism of the moment struck me. Even the C-46 itself seemed vaguely restless.

Suddenly the plane veered sharply left. The captain yanked off his oxygen mask. "Holy Hell!" he shouted.

I looked past him and saw out the left window a trio of motionless paddles where propellers should be whirling. The red oil pressure light confirmed complete engine failure.

Sitting erect, the pilot yelled, "No chance to restart this bastard." He feathered the props, shut off the gas, turned off the switches, and came to an idle cutoff. He threw out his arm and yelled, "Help me trim her. Tell the radio operator to call a Mayday. Quick! Quick! And for Chrissake, fasten your chute."

I was shocked at how scared he looked. I'd flown with him once before and judged him to be cool under pressure. I was wrong.

We were losing altitude at 200 feet per minute. In spite of the cold, my hands were wet. I felt the eerie silence of the missing engine. Suddenly, my mind flashed home. Where was Amy at this moment?

"I'm taking this bastard into Yunnanyi," he barked. "Without hydraulics, it'll take us both to land her, so I want you to get your ass into it. Goddamit, are you listening? Better say your Goddamned prayers when we reach the ridge."

The radio operator came into the cockpit. "Air Traffic Control has directed us to land at Baker Jig."

The pilot threw up his arms. "Where in the hell do they think I'm headed?" he yelled. "Think I'm out for a joy ride?" He turned and shoved him. "Get the hell back there to your radio." He was a madman.

Fortunately, the night was clear and we were empty. With the biggest sigh of my life, I looked back at the ridge marking the Yunnanyi region. We must have had all of two hundred feet to spare.

The pilot turned to me. "If you think you wanna help," he said sarcastically, "get ready to handle the flaps and the landing gear when I tell you. And I mean immediately when I tell you." He ripped off his oxygen mask and tossed it aside.

I gazed at him; fear blazed in his eyes.

When they had Yunnanyi in their view, he said, "If you think you can handle it and if you're not too Goddamned busy, see if you can raise the Baker Jig tower."

"Baker Jig, this is five-nine-seven. Over."

I guess my voice didn't suit him. At the top of his voice he yelled, "Christ, can't you do anything? Give me that fucking radio." He grabbed it from me.

"Baker Jig, five-nine-seven. We're on single engine."

"Roger, five-nine-seven, we have you. What is your position now? Over."

I sat and looked straight ahead, afraid I'd antagonize him by looking at him. I prayed he'd hold together long enough to set the plane down.

"Forty miles east on Charlie course," he answered the tower.

"Roger. Wind 280 degrees at twenty miles an hour, barometric pressure 29.98. We'll keep traffic clear for you."

"You sure as hell better. We're going to make a straight-in approach."

I reached to the panel to set the altimeter. He pushed my hand away with a jerk. "I changed my mind about you helping me to land. You weak-kneed son of a bitch, I want you to sit there and not do a Goddamned thing. Do you understand?"

I nodded.

"Jesus, take your Goddamned mask off and strap your chute on. You act as though it's your first trip."

My head pounded. I gave another fleeting thought to Amy and Mother. Suddenly I heard an ominous blare from the radio.

"C-87 on approach, do not land!" The tower operator's voice was tremulous. "Repeat. Do not land. We have a plane on Mayday."

"Jesus Christ," the captain shrieked. I thought he was going to cry.

"Baker Jig, tell that fucking 87 to get out of the area. I'll have your ass if he isn't clear in one minute."

A few tense minutes crept by like an hour.

"Five-niner-seven." The tower operator's voice was high and frantic. "Five-niner-seven, you cannot land. You cannot land here. A C-87 cracked up on the runway. You cannot land."

I felt hot around my ears, my neck, my face. My throat was tight. Vivid images flashed through my mind -- Father in his wheel chair, Amy and I at the movies, Mother in the cellar washing.

I looked at the pilot. A metamorphosis was occurring. He took his hands off the pedestal, sat back in his seat and exhaled loudly. He stared straight ahead. Was he reconciled to crashing? Had he given up? I took over the controls.

Sweat broke out on my face. On single engine, we couldn't land, couldn't climb, and we were too low now to bail out. I had only one option: I'd take over completely, defy the tower and land along side the strip, using the runway lights as a guide. Perhaps I could keep one wheel on the strip.

Suddenly, I remembered a sketch I'd made in my notebook for an emergency. Just north of the Yannanyi traffic pattern was a field once used by the Flying Tigers. The strip probably wasn't long enough for a C-46, but it was something.

I grabbed the radio. "Baker Jig, are there lights on the auxiliary field just north of you? Can you call them?"

"Not certain about the lights. Stand by."

"Okay," I said, not sure the captain was listening, "we're a minute away." He said nothing.

Twenty seconds to landing. "This is it," I said, "we're over Yunnanyi." My heart raced. We were on the downwind leg. I saw the C-87 sprawled across the runway like a wounded bird.

Suddenly, miraculously, ten seconds before I had to turn onto Yunnanyi's base leg, the lights came on at the fighter strip, each light a precious jewel. I yelled, "Thank God for the Flying Tigers!"

The BJ tower came on. "Good luck, five-niner-seven."

The captain was silent. I looked hard at him. "Do you want me to take her in?" I wasn't sure which answer I preferred.

He sat up. "No, I'm all right now." His voice was even and low. "Just give me a hand with the pedestal."

Could I trust him? If he came in too high or too hot or not lined up, I'd overpower him on the controls. If his speed was wrong, I'd push his hand off the throttles.

"I think we'll go straight in," he said.

"No, no," I said. "We can hold altitude and they're no hills to the north. We're practically on the downwind leg now. We'll make a normal approach. Let's try to land in the first hundred feet."

"Okay."

I dropped the gear and the flaps, full. He applied power to compensate.

In thirty seconds, we turned left onto the base leg, then left again onto the approach. Without much help from me, he lined up well and stalled it in a perfect three-point landing at the very end of the strip. It took both of us to keep from rolling to the left. The end of the strip was coming up fast. My heart was pounding. Oh no, I thought, not after all this!

With just a couple hundred feet left, he let the plane run off the strip to the left. Fortunately, our speed had dissipated and we rolled to a stop. The left wing tip buried itself into the mud. He shut off the engine and we ran to the cabin door and hurried down the ladder.

Two jeeps sped out. The base CO shook our hands.

"Good job, men. I'm glad we were around to put the lights on. We'll get you over to Baker Jig right away."

Tension between the captain and me began immediately on the jeep ride.

"That was a close one," the captain said. "You're a great copilot. I don't know what I woulda done without you."

"Okay," was all I said.

He became ebullient. I'd have no part of that. If he feared I'd report his behavior, he needn't have worried. There was no procedure for this, and copilots' opinions were never solicited. But I knew this: I would refuse to fly with him again.

I had no idea where we'd spend the night. Yunnanyi said they had no place for us, so after two hours we were on a C-46, deadheading back to Kunming. Luckily for us, I guess, there was a plane ready for flight back to Chabua when the pilot became sick to the stomach. We substituted for the crew. It was a strained flight. The captain wanted to talk, I didn't. We landed in Chabua at three in the morning. I walked directly to the dispensary for my two shots of Old Crow. If I ever needed them, it was then.

I flew three more flights in December, all uneventful. I wasn't scheduled to fly on Christmas, but it wouldn't have mattered. Except for a few carols and a Christmas message in church, there was absolutely no evidence anywhere on the base of the saddest day of the year for men away from home. You'd think someone would have fashioned and decorated a tree, or put up red and green streamers, or sung carols or the sad lament "I'll be home for Christmas." My morale hit bottom.

The Worst Day

The weather was on my mind a lot, especially on nights before scheduled flights. Most winter days were partly sunny and warm on the base, but that wasn't what counted. Look east and you'd see a batch of ominous clouds hovering like vultures over the First Ridge, a few fighting to be the highest and meanest of the lot.

Here under the roof of the world, treacherous weather resulted from the clashing of three mighty Eurasian air masses -- lows moving west along the main ranges of the Himalayas, highs from the Bay of Bengal, and more lows from Siberia. The constant churning of these systems produced the absolute worst flying conditions -- violent turbulence, severe icing, hazardous downdrafts, howling, angry winds, pounding rain, sleet and hail, blinding snowstorms, slicing wind shear, brilliant lightning followed by deafening thunder, scary St. Elmo's fire dancing off props.

I was scheduled to fly early on January 6, 1945, a day which became famous in the history of the Hump. Before I pulled down my mosquito bar and tucked myself in the night before, I moseyed out of the basha to take one last peek at the sky to the east. It was normal, mostly clear but with the usual cumulus clouds standing like night watchmen over the First Ridge.

Out of bed early the next day, I sensed a change. During the night, the world of the Hump had become something strange and foreign, never seen before. I was scheduled to fly with Captain Henry (unfortunately I didn't record his first name), a tall, soft-spoken, friendly guy, a big smile his trademark. Living in the same basha, we met and walked to the officers' mess, then to operations.

A huge gun-metal gray lid tightly covered the morning sky.

"I thought I'd have to wait till spring to see the monsoon," I said.

"No, this isn't a monsoon sky," he said, surveying the whole expanse. "Frankly, I don't like the looks of it."

We filed a flight plan for Chanyi and took off on C-46 number 634. Immediately we hit severe turbulence, both of us grabbing the control column as we climbed for Moran. We turned on both radio compasses; the needles spun like roulette wheels. We struggled to reach seven thousand feet.

"We must be over the station by now," Henry said. "I'll take her up to ten thousand feet before we head out." The rain and sleet hit the fuselage so hard he had to shout to be heard.

Suddenly we hit an iron wall of even heavier rain, jolting us back in our seats. Ice was forming on the wings and the props. The right engine coughed. Henry put on carburetor heat. I strapped on my chute.

The first radio checkpoint was Shingbwiyang, Burma, ninety miles from Moran, north of our route, off our left wing tip as we passed. Never a powerful signal, it didn't come in at all.

"We'll take an aural null," Captain Henry said, reaching to the ceiling, switching the frequency to 1625, and slowly cranking the antenna. When he found the beacon, the static in our headsets disappeared.

"My God, Carl, Shingbwiyang's straight ahead! We're forty miles north of our course!" He threw the plane sharply right. "Okay, I'm heading southeast till we get to Tingkawsakan. Then we'll talk it over."

The turbulence grew worse, tossing the C-46 about wildly. I thought back to my aborted first flight in November. I caught a glimpse of thick ice on the wings and of hail like golf balls striking everywhere. Nothing we could do about the wing ice, the deicer boots having been damaged and removed. But the prop deicers were functioning, slinging huge clumps of ice against the fuselage. My eyes shot open wide when I heard the first volley. The windshield too was icing up. The air speed jumped from 80 to 260 and back down again as sharp gusts pushed us up, then down, then sideways. Lose the artificial horizon and we'd have no idea whether we were upside down or right side up.

We took another null and calculated we'd just crossed Tingkawksakan. "I'm going to hold 150 degrees until we pass Myitkyana. Check for a null in a few minutes."

I was as scared as I'd been a month ago when we lost an engine, but this time I wasn't thinking of death or Amy or my folks. I was too busy, too involved. And this time I had a supremely confident pilot.

When the null showed Myitkyina off our right wing tip, Henry said, "Okay, it sounds crazy, but we know the wind is directly out of the south at more than a hundred. I'm going to make the biggest correction you've ever seen." After a minute he said, "You're in this thing too. What do ya think?"

I agreed. "I was taught to trust my instruments. And anyway, I'd rather end up south over Burma than mess with those giant peaks in the north." With our nose sticking 30 degrees south of our course, we crabbed sideways to Paoshan.

We had a respite of about fifteen minutes -- bumpy gusts, but not violent. Suddenly, we hit a downdraft and heard a loud crack. The radio operator, I figured. I went back to check. His head had struck the ceiling, but fortunately he was okay. In the cabin I saw a few drums of gasoline had broken loose. Potential disaster.

Henry shoved the throttles full forward and the mixture control full rich to try to hold altitude. It didn't help; we were in God's hands. Inexplicably, after losing 4000 feet we began rising, somewhere, I must believe, safely and miraculously tucked away in a tiny valley between mountain peaks a thousand feet higher just north and south of us.

The radio operator came to the cockpit to tell us he'd heard five Maydays -- planes lost, desperately seeking a fix, planes reporting lost engines, crews about to bail out. Suddenly I felt an occult, out-of-body experience, a sense of calm, of peace, as though we were spectators to the drama and danger all around us, benignly and mystically watched over by a higher force.

We crossed over Paoshan and turned left to 120 degrees, still keeping that tremendous 30-degree correction. The Paoshan to Kunming leg covered two hundred thirty statute miles, about fifty-five minutes with the usual tailwind. It would be longer today. I said a prayer that the rest of our trip would be safe. Make it to Kunming, I told myself, then a 10-minute flight north to Chanyi, and we'd remain overnight. Certainly they'd close the Hump today.

As we approached Kunming, we saw the flares of their Very gun, shot up to help lost planes home in. We passed Kunming and flew north to Chanyi.

We held over Chanyi for a plane beneath us, broke out of the scud a hundred feet above the ground and put down in a fierce crosswind, halfway between a wheel landing and three-points. Any landing you walk away from is a good one, we learned somewhere along the line.

We looked at each other, smiled, and, simultaneously, exhaled loudly and laughed. The radio operator came up to congratulate us on our creative navigation. We taxied and parked and walked through the rain to operations.

"Where do we sleep, captain?" Henry asked the operations officer.

"You're not going to believe this, but I'm not authorized to allow you to remain over night."

"Who the hell is?" Henry asked. "We can't go back in this stuff. What about the guys at Kunming?"

"It's the same story. Everyone must go back."

"And if we don't?" he asked. Not really an option, we both knew.

We ate our eggs and bread, drank our strong coffee, returned to operations and stormed about restlessly. I thought about faking a Form One report on 634 that might ground it. But I didn't suggest it. For the second time in one day, we'd have to fly into the jaws of death in the worst weather the Hump had ever had.

Once our fate was cast, we stopped bitching and talked over our plan. There were two separate problems, one navigational, the other operational. We'd manage the first by taking aural nulls at Yunnanyi, Yungling, and Shingbwiyang, and unless they told us something different, we'd maintain a 30-degree correction. As for the severe turbulence and icing in the storms, we'd both hang on to the controls and use our throttles, carburetor heat, and mixture controls as we thought best at the time. Luck and skill would both be involved. I'd do one more thing. I'd continue to pray.

If we hoped for calmer conditions on the flight west, we were immediately brought back to reality. No sooner were we airborne than the storm's full fury struck -- banging, violent turbulence, howling rain and sleet, frightening thunder and lightning. Climbing to altitude was tortuously slow, even though we were empty. As we climbed, ice again flew off the props and hit the fuselage with ear-splitting clangs.

We heard desperate Maydays from crews completely lost, far to the north, almost certainly. The nulls confirmed that the wind continued steady out of the south. We estimated the speed at 100, maybe 120, miles per hour. Except for one little hiccup, the engines were functioning well, thank God.

After four tense hours, we'd run out of daylight. Chabua tower cleared us for landing. A strong gust lifted our right wing, but we put the plane down safely and taxied in. Our nightmare was over.

In the dispensary we toasted our survival with Old Crow, then staggered down the road to the mess hall. We ate quickly and hoofed back to the basha.

The scuttlebutt started immediately. Who was out today, who didn't return, how many planes were lost? I had a hard time settling down. Finally, grateful to be alive, I lay down to pleasant dreams, dreams of home, of Amy, of the start of a new life.

After a peaceful sleep, I awoke two hours later than usual the next morning. The officers' mess buzzed with questions and rumors. Even though the weather had not improved, planes were taking off. I shrugged my shoulders. At least I didn't have to face that killer storm again.

Captain Henry and I had flown to China in daylight, and, except for an hour, back to India in daylight that fateful day. I was puzzled and a bit annoyed to hear about the storm THAT NIGHT. What about the two DAYS of the storm? But that was nothing compared to the shock of hearing old Hump pilots after the war talking about the night the Hump was closed.

Really, someone closed the Hump? Not for Captain Henry and me they didn't. I heard later that our Chabua commander, Col. C. F. Skannal, had, in fact, closed down operations. The mystery deepened when I read in General Tunner's book *Over the Hump* that when he took over command five months earlier he issued an order "to the effect that weather was a factor which every Operations Officer would consider in dispatching aircraft," in essence countermanding his own dictum "The Hump is never closed." I find it astounding that I flew the Hump for nearly one year and never knew that weather was to be considered in dispatching planes. When Henry and I left Chabua that morning, no one knew how bad conditions were, but by the time we and other planes landed in China, everyone must have known. Why was it, then, that if weather was to be a considered in dispatching flights, and if we asked to remain over night, we were forced to return to India?

In his book General Tunner wrote, "When a pilot flew into a particularly severe storm, found his plane being buffeted around and icing up to the extent that he might just not make it, that man had my orders to turn around and come back." Ordered to return? Why didn't we know that? Had I known, I doubt that we would have turned back anyway -- flying the wrong direction on a one-way street, on instruments, in severe turbulence and ice, perhaps with engine trouble?

No, no. If conditions over the whole Hump were unsafe for anyone, they were unsafe for everyone. General Tunner's headquarters should have called the shot. According to Downie, by the afternoon of the second day, accident statistics had shown up in headquarters and flights were officially canceled for the first time since General Hardin's "no weather" proclamation had been issued in December of 1943. The new directive became, "The Hump is never closed, usually."

I was amazed to read accounts of pilots considering turning back on January 6-7 or putting in at fields short of their destination. Neither of those ideas crossed our minds. And I was astounded to read how long it took some pilots to realize the wind was in fact coming out of the south, not the west, and at more than 100 miles per hour, not the relatively benign 60 to 70 of the prevailing west wind. We were all busy struggling with severe turbulence and ice. But we had to know where we were. I'm shocked that not a single account I read mentioned the ultimate dependable radio navigation aid all pilots learned in training, the aural null. Thank God for Captain Henry.

Had I been a first pilot flying with a green copilot that day, would I have had the courage to make so big a course correction? One thing's certain. Those crews who did not call on their training and did not trust their instruments are resting in the Himalayas, far to the north.

I was curious about the weather phenomenon responsible for the January 6-7 catastrophe. A staff sergeant in operations who appeared to have the best grasp of the vagaries of Hump weather told me that a dense occluded front had moved across Africa and India, picked up moisture in the Bay of Bengal and sped east to Assam, arriving in the early morning. From pilot reports, he concluded there must have been winds shifting from all points of the compass at speeds as high as 150mph and vertical currents more than 200mph. Cloud tops reached 40,000 feet.

Walking away from operations, I shook my head. How lucky to be here.

How bad was January 6-7, 1945? There's no one authoritative source for statistics. At Chabua, we heard that thirteen planes were lost all told. According to General Tunner, ATC lost nine planes, eighteen crew members, and nine passengers. If a report is true that all three CNAC transports out that day were lost, as were three belonging to American tactical commands, fifteen would seem to be the best account. Even up to today, I suspect January 6-7, 1945, is listed in the annals of the Air Force as the worst day's loss of aircraft due to bad weather anywhere in the world.

There's a sad postscript to this story. One bright sunny day a few weeks later, Captain Henry, this brilliant pilot of what I will remember as flight 634, this great, friendly guy, took off for China and was never heard from again. I will not forget his smile.

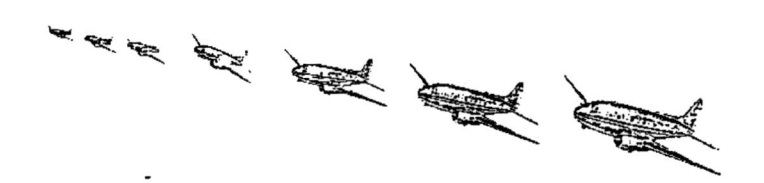

Carl F. Constein

Visiting Mighty Everest's Cousins

I flew copilot for several hot-shot jockeys who were frustrated by their assignment, pilots who never got over their cadet dreams of flying bombers. It's true, flying C-46s was not thrilling. Think of it as driving a truck -- except on those flights when you lose an engine, or when you're caught in a severe storm, or when you land with a low ceiling, or when the wayward west wind trips you up and blows hard out of the south.

A few weeks after the terror of January 6, I rode shotgun for a fellow who was also out on the Hump that fateful day. Admitting he was probably too far north of course that day, he got to wondering, he said, what it's like with the four-mile-high big boys of the Himalayas.

On the northern edge of the map, he had spotted, as I had, two black spots of concentric circles -- marked 23,000 feet! Returning from Kunming, I noticed we began inching north, the compass eventually reading 310 degrees.

I nudged him. "What's the deal?"

"I'm going to check out Everest's cousins up here. Okay with you?"

I knew I was stuck. I shrugged and made a face.

After thirty minutes we were a hundred miles north of the Charlie course, heading for a place called Likiang, China. We were flying at 19,000 feet, the first of the two colossuses, Yulung, looming just ahead. I worried the guy would take us so close we'd lose control in the mighty currents of permanent windstorms. I was right to be worried, and I was scared. The plane bounced around like a ball. It took both of us to keep from flipping over -- an eerie feeling on this clear, beautiful day. I stared in awe at the top of the peak, 4000 feet above.

My stomach was in a knot. "Let's get the hell out of here," I called out.

He smiled. "Okay. I just wanted to satisfy my curiosity."

He took a southwest heading, passed Ft. Hertz and, flying on Contact Flight Rules, descending gradually, we arrived at Chabua and landed, tanks nearly bone dry. One more strange flight with one more strange pilot.

A few days later, I got to thinking about the Yunglung experience. I shuddered. Another minute in that windstorm and we'd have been goners. We'd have been one more statistic, one more plane missing, this one farther north than anyone would dream of searching.

Was anyone assigned to search for missing planes?

In a handsome, significant book entitled *Flying the Hump*, Don Downie writes about a search and rescue unit. The impetus, he says, was the August, 1943, bail-out of high-ranking Chinese officers, an American adviser to General Stilwell, and Eric Severeid, distinguished CBS war correspondent. Within two hours, a C-47 had dropped vital supplies into the bail-out area, and later a flight surgeon parachuted in. Sixteen days later a ground rescue mission reached the Burma village where the survivors waited.

Other sporadic rescue efforts were made following that rescue. Then a Captain "Blackie" Porter was appointed Air

Rescue Officer with his base in Chabua. He recruited three other pilots and ten enlisted men, scrounged two old C-47s, and resurrected two B-25s from a salvage yard. An L-5 Grasshopper completed the motley force.

Writing in *Over the Hump,* General Tunner gives this account. Before he took over in August, 1944, "a few dedicated men were carrying on a cowboy operation under the very general supervision of the wing commander at Chabua. Though brave and hard-working, the members of the unit just didn't have the authority to conduct operations in an efficient manner." Washington approved Tunner's plan to have one agency, the India-China Division, conduct search and rescue. Operating out of Mohanbari, the unit started with twelve officers and twenty-four enlisted men; within a month the strength was doubled and four B-25s, a C-47, and an L-5 assigned.

It isn't clear whether some of these planes were the same ones from the earlier rescue unit in Chabua. What is clear is this: not only did I never see any of these planes, I never knew of their existence -- this in spite of the monthly bulletin Tunner said the unit put out, which I also never saw. "It was obvious now," General Tunner writes, "that the Search and Rescue Unit was operating on an efficient, business-like basis. Surely this lessened some of the qualms on the men flying the Hump."

It might have helped my morale, had I known. If only someone would have rescued Captain Henry, to whom I owe so much. Five hundred-ninety planes carrying 2,380 crewmen were reported missing over the Hump. eleven hundred seventy-one men were saved and 1,314 were confirmed dead. Of those who survived the crashes and bail-outs, a high percentage were rescued.

I know now there was a search and rescue unit. After the war, pilots from other bases in Assam told me they had seen a blue and yellow C-47 rescue plane with "Somewhere I'll Find You" painted on its nose. Having tried to learn everything I could at Chabua, I'm flabbergasted that I never even heard of it.

Walt Carre from Mullica Hills, New Jersey, a B-24 crew chief with the Seventh Bomb Group in Myitkyina, told me an intriguing tale of the first helicopter rescue over the Hump. A B-25 went down in the Burma jungle in January, 1945. Walt's group wired Wright Field in Dayton, Ohio, for help. Within seventy-four hours, a C-54 delivered a disassembled chopper. Meanwhile, the B-25 crew had walked out. Before leaving, the stateside helicopter pilot trained a pilot from Walt's group to fly it.

A few months later, the helicopter was used for the first time. A mechanic somewhere in China had accidentally shot himself in the hand. The chopper plucked him off the mountain and flew him to a field hospital for treatment.

Walt's first-born was born at this time. To mark her birth, he painted her name and birth date on the copter that pulled off the rescue. "Whenever I saw a chopper around after that," he said, "I looked for her name."

The only bail-out survivor I knew was a pilot from my basha. After he was missing for a couple months, we pretty well gave up hope of ever seeing him again. But he did return, and he told us a fascinating story. Injured, he was cared for by Kachin natives for six weeks. When he was well enough to walk, they escorted him to a rescue point. Before he left, the chief gave him a going-away present -- a brand new Japanese camera!

I never bailed out and therefore never needed rescue, thank God, but I came close to jumping on two occasions when we were on Mayday. I certainly felt like it a few times, more out of frustration than danger when I flew copilot for a squadron of Service pilots.

In February, my friends Fettelah, Hennehan, and two other long-time copilots and I were ordered to Myitkyina, Burma, for two weeks of detached service. After Stilwell recaptured Myitkyina from the Japanese in August, 1944, ATC brought in a squadron of civilian pilots to fly cargo directly to Kunming on a more southerly route. Brand-new in the Air Corps, little total time, checked out on the C-47 just before ferrying them here, they needed help on familiarization with routes, elevations, landing procedures on China's fields.

I had an uneasy feeling about these Service pilots, an S on their wings, and for a reason. They were the epitome of the hot pilot -- cocky, reveling in their new status, proud of their ratings as C-47 pilots. Some of them had fewer than a hundred hours total time in the service. From day one their attitude was, hell, who needs help? The weather? Not that bad, they said.

Fortunately, it's hard to make a mistake in the good old Gonney Bird, but these guys had me scared half to death during landings. I shook my head when I thought of them in a C-46. By the end of my two weeks in Myitkyina, I was eager to get out of there. I couldn't have imagined this, but I was even eager to get back to the C-46.

Control of Burma allowed additional Hump routes. The Douglass four-engine DC-4 Skymaster came on line in 1942. The Air Force immediately adapted it for transport service, giving it the designation C-54. It was faster than the C-46 and had a seventy percent greater payload, but its ceiling was limited. From their base in Tezgaon in east Bengal, C-54s flew due east across Burma, then turned north into Kunming. Their altitude was 10,000 feet going east, no higher than 12,000 returning. Some old C-46 pilots called it the milk run.

I breathed a big sigh of relief when I got back to Chabua, my home away from home. I now had enough time and was gung ho to check out as left-seat pilot. But Chabua needed more copilots than first pilots, and my request was put on hold. I flew a hundred nine hours in February, all the flights but one unremarkable.

The guy I flew with the day I ticked off as remarkable displayed the same cockiness as the Service pilots I'd just left in Burma. At the end of the day I was convinced he should never have been given his wings.

It was a day for instrument flying. The weatherman gave us a wind out of the southwest at 70mph. The wind speed was about average but the direction may have been just a bit more southerly than normal. After leaving Moran, he made a 10-degree correction to the south. Perhaps, I thought, he flew on January 6 and had that strong southerly wind on his mind. I told him he was making too big a correction. He resented my suggestion that we take radio compass bearings en route. When he finally did, we were too far away to receive any signals at all. Too proud to admit he was lost, he refused to call a Mayday. Finally he had no choice and made the call. Even then, rather than confessing he had no idea where the devil he was, he used the old Air Corps euphemism "uncertain of my position." Stations in the area took radio fixes and gave us a heading of 300 degrees. We limped into Kunming, gas tanks nearly empty.

After we landed I went into operations to learn where we were when we got our fix. I shivered at the answer. We'd been flying a hundred miles south, over Japanese-held territory!

The irony struck me. In spite of his stupidity and arrogance, this guy probably made his time and got home. Captain Henry, a paragon of a pilot, is only a memory. Whatever happened on his ill-fated flight must have been beyond human control.

In March I was ordered to Gaya, India, together with my friends Fox, Davis, and Fettelah, for training and check out as first pilot. There was none of the tension of checkrides in cadet training. We shot a lot of landings, had a few simulated single engines and IFR landings. There at sea level, six hundred miles west of Chabua, flying empty planes, it was all so easy, almost fun.

I have pleasant memories of five days in Gaya. I recall living in a large brick-floored tent, clean and well-maintained. The food was good. There was a full moon while I was there, and I can still picture the flat expansive landscape and hear the exotic midnight chanting celebrating a Hindu religious festival.

Gaya marked an important break in my Hump service. About halfway to meeting the flight-time requirement, I'd have to hang in for another four months or so. Now that I'd be flying from the left seat, I'd have more control of my own fate. So far so good; would my luck hold out?

Of Nudes and Seals

Gaya was refreshing, a vacation away from the job, but I was glad to be back in Chabua, eager to earn that coveted ticket to the states. When I'd arrived in Chabua, the flight time requirement was six hundred fifty hours, but in his wisdom General Tunner raised it a hundred hours, for pilot safety, he averred. Baloney, the pilots responded, and morale took another nose dive.

I was overjoyed to find two V-mail letters from Amy waiting for me. She always had small talk and home-front goodies for me, but the thrill was in holding her letters in my hand, delighting in the graceful hand-writing, rushing to the end for the loving words I knew were waiting.

I sat down immediately and answered, relating my relaxed time at Gaya, describing the enchanting midnight music wafting across the plain. I spoke about the future. D-day past, the end of the war in Europe was a matter of time. Less certain was the war with Japan, but I was optimistic that once I got home I would not be sent overseas again. I went overboard in my enthusiasm for the future and my hopes and dreams.

My first trip as pilot went off without a hitch. After a few more, I felt comfortable in the left seat, not only flying the plane but as boss, as captain. I resolved I wouldn't make foolhardy excursions off the course, and I wouldn't lose my cool and take out my own weaknesses on the copilot. I'd treat my copilots as friends, and I'd seek their help. Captain Henry would be my model.

A few weeks after I started flying left seat, the monsoon blew in off the Indian Ocean, making its semi-annual switch from northeast to southwest, adding its nasty mix to the air mass heavyweights jabbing and punching incessantly. It rained every single day, more than a hundred inches a year, flooding the huge delta. Assam became a dank, simmering flatland. Everywhere, everyday, the mud was thick as goo. We no longer walked to the flight line.

The monsoon brought an unchanging cloud cover, an immense gray tent, forcing us to fly on instruments until we broke out over the top. Inside the tent, invisible storms lurked like assassins in waiting, not as intense as winter storms but always a threat, always harboring ice.

I preferred winter. On the base, the temperature was moderate and the air clean and invigorating. The Hump itself was free of the boring overcast which hid my wished-for view of the mountains and the jungles. And the clouds of winter -- a magnificent kaleidoscope. The cumulonimbus were king of the beasts, high and mighty, stable, fearsome. Others were phantasmagorial, an art deco skyscraper one moment, a map of Europe the next, a Roman god then a denizen of the deep. I reveled in the sight.

When I finally left India, I took home this fascination with clouds. My winter tennis buddies in Florida consider me a weather mavin, counting on me for predictions.

The monsoon was hard on everyone. General Tunner speaks of other causes of the Command's fourth-rate morale -- shortages of such basic items as razor blades, candy, soft drinks, entertainment and recreation, fresh food, good water. And disease. The flood plain of the Brahmaputra River was prime breeding ground for the mosquito; malaria, diarrhea, and dysentery were prevalent.

"Next to the combat soldier in the foxhole," Tunner wrote, "these poor guys in their thatched bashas were about as bad off as a man in the service could get."

Hyperbole, I'd say. I thought of myself as fortunate to have a comfortable bed to return to every day. Morale has to do with little things. I would have liked to have a daily, at least a weekly, newspaper. I would have liked to visit the cities of China. I would have liked a safer airplane. I would have liked to know there were real live people in charge on the base, officers who cared about their men and could explain their orders. And I would have liked at least some fresh food.

The mess officer said he could solve that problem. If we put in an extra rupee a day for dinner, he'd serve us fresh vegetables. Of course, we said, as we coughed up our seven rupees for the first week.

Monday came. Along with the usual canned meat and vegetables, we saw on the table cucumber and onion salad. Delicious. The next day, again, cucumber and onion salad. Okay, let's give him a chance, we said. You guessed it-- cucumber and onion salad was all there was. We were had.

After nearly sixty years, there are some details I can't recall about life in Chabua. In his book General Tunner said he tried to boost morale by sending entertainers like singer Tony Martin and the up-and-coming concert pianist Leonard Pennario around the circuit to entertain us. Not while I was there, sir; *that* I would recall. In fact, I don't remember a USO troupe or any entertainment at all. Were there movies? I don't recall seeing one.

I do recall a few adventures off the base. It wasn't easy, but one day a few of us requisitioned a jeep to drive into Dibrugarh, the closest town. I can picture the dirt street lined with merchants, teeth stained by betel nuts, hawking silver filigree bracelets fashioned by craftsmen sitting cross-legged over their small charcoal furnaces.

I still shudder at the grating of the merchants' guttural, non-stop chatter. I recall wrinkling up my nose at the miserable fruits and vegetables in the market, and I can still smell the indescribable odors. Most memorable of all, I recall making way in the market for a cow, a sacred cow, her body covered with ugly sores and hundreds of buzzing flies. Poverty and squalor took on a new meaning.

Dibrubarh was in Assam province. After the war, the Sylhet district of Assam, together with the East Bengal province, became East Pakistan, Then in 1971, separated from West Pakistan by the full expanse of India, it seceded and became its own country of Bangladesh. Predominantly Muslim, it is one of the poorest countries in the world, vulnerable to floods (a half-million people died in the flood of 1970) and cyclones.

India is predominantly Hindu; the caste system was very much alive in 1945. Our basha had a wet sweeper and a dry sweeper. When the wet sweeper took off on a drunken binge, the CO searched in Dibrugarh for a replacement. There were none to be had, none that low. He was forced to send a plane to Calcutta to pick one up.

Life on the base went on in its own boring pace, excitement coming in unexpected ways. A crisis developed over the nudes on the walls of the officers' club, the venue for church services. The chaplain complained that the murals were inappropriate and distracting. I attended church once a month or so; I saw his point. When he persisted and demanded the murals be removed, a brouhaha erupted. Absolutely not, the men said. But the chaplain had clout from above -- brass, not heavenly intervention -- and forced a compromise. The CO's people would design a circus theme, keeping the nudes but covering them with curtains on Sundays.

The club was transformed into a Big Top, parachutes billowing from the ceiling. But someone either goofed or reneged: the nudes were painted over, and circus animals replaced them. You wouldn't believe the brawl. The rec officer had the chutzpah to schedule a meeting to try to bring peace. He was shouted down and walked out in disgust.

My favorite memory of the caper was the tirade of the little Italian guy who appointed himself spokesman for the pilots. "Yes," he conceded, "we did agree to the redecoration, but only after you bastards promised to keep our luscious nudes. Now what in the hell do we have? We have a bunch of bare-assed seals." Some phrases live on.

The spiritual lost to the carnal. Church attendance fell twenty-five percent.

Meanwhile, I was doing okay in the left seat. But whether you're a pilot, a pro golfer, or an opera star, you can't give a perfect performance every time. I took off late one night for Kunming, with a partial load to be dropped off at Myitkyina, Burma, the base where I had just recently spent two weeks on detached service.

We climbed to 7,000 feet over Moran and, continuing our ascent, headed east over the First Ridge. In a half-hour we spotted the lights of Myitkyina and prepared to land. Of course I knew the field and its elevation well. Even so, I came in very high on the final approach.

My copilot was a veteran Hump pilot who'd been demoted because he had a taxi accident. Crash a plane and walk away -- that's okay. But hit the wing tip of a parked plane while you are taxiing, and you get a black mark on your personnel record. The buggers might even attach your salary to pay for the repair.

The copilot said, "Put her down, don't go around." I put her down all right: I dropped the sucker in a three-point stall from fifteen feet! Thank God it was the old workhorse C-46. Not many planes will take that abuse.

I walked into operations with my head down. I reddened when I looked up and saw a face from home -- Robert Angstadt, the chief pilot of our childhood Walter Mitty caper in his father's garage. What a coincidence to run into someone from Fleetwood. What a joyous reunion. We reminisced a bit then chatted a long time -- where we trained, where we'd been, our families, when we expected to go home.

After the Myitkyina cargo was offloaded, I strode out to the tarmac, happy to have seen Robert, thankful that if he had heard about my terrible landing, the worst of my career, he was gracious enough to ignore it.

But there was still my pride to consider. I felt sheepish. Should I say something to the copilot about my landing? Would I have gone around if he hadn't spoken up? Better just shut up.

We took off for China. As we approached the Kunming control, my stomach churned a bit. I thought I detected concern on the part of the copilot. My self-esteem required a velvety landing.

I expelled a loud sigh of relief as the wheels touched down, the landing smooth as silk.

We walked into operations and, as we always did when we arrived in China late at night, staked out an empty spot on the floor to get some shuteye while the plane was being unloaded. I was no sooner asleep than I felt a stinging kick on the sole of my foot. I jumped up, ready to throw a punch. There stood this grizzled pilot spieling a quaint foreign tongue. It wasn't Chinese. I'll give it to you phonetically.

"Sawck, Constein! Waas gate awe dough?" Say, Constein! What's going on here?

Talk about shock! Twelve thousand miles from home, one Pennsylvania Dutch Hump pilot recognized another lying on the floor sound asleep. Incredible! And just a couple hours earlier I'd run into another friend from home.

George Wenrich and I had been classmates at Kutztown State Teachers College. We reminisced and talked about the future. He planned to go to law school, he said. Our lively confab ended when he was called to report to his plane.

"Mock's gute," he said, smiling broadly as he walked out of operations. "Make it good, good luck."

It was 0300 before my crew and I left Kunming. The night was crystal clear, the moon nearly full, the sky ablaze, lit by precious stones. Off in the west, somewhere near the First Ridge, we saw flashes of lightning, as pretty as fireworks.

Halfway across the Hump, I pointed and said to the copilot, "Those cumulonimbus don't look that high. I'm going to go over them."

"You'll never do it," he said sardonically.

We were flying at 19,000 feet. I applied power and began a slow climb. In a half-hour we were at 23,000, as high as I'd ever been. I looked over at the copilot. He was a poker face. We were about a hundred miles from the thunderheads, as angry looking as any I'd ever seen.

Not at all sure of myself, I continued climbing. I just didn't feel up to facing a thunderstorm tonight.

We reached 26,000, and I struggled for more. In ten minutes I faced reality: we were not going to get over those monsters. Would it be better to descend a bit or hold my altitude before I flew into them? How could I know?

In five minutes we hit the leading edge of the line. The storm's fury struck with violent turbulence, howling wind and hail pushing us one way then another. With the Aldis lamp for light, I looked out and was startled to see ice forming so soon -- on the wings and around the carburetor scoops.

"I'll help you with the carburetor heat and the mixture," the copilot said. "You take care of the throttles." When a super gust of wind nearly tipped us over, he grabbed his control column with his strong arms to help me control the ship.

After a long ten minutes, we broke out on the Assam side. Having used so much fuel to climb, we had a new problem: the gas tank gauges were touching the empty mark. I started my descent.

"Better put the gear down so the engines stay warm."

Wanting to save fuel, I thought I could avoid that.

Within range of Chabua, without waiting for my instructions, he called the tower. "Victor George, this is zero-seven-two. We're low on fuel. Request straight-in approach. Over."

"Roger, you are number one for landing."

Thank God for that, I said to myself. Thank God there's no ceiling. I prayed that the fuel would last.

We landed and turned off the runway. I exhaled loudly and threw up my arms. I hoped the fuel would hold out until we got to the revetment; my pride had been wounded enough for one day.

After I shut the plane down, I said, "I know what you're thinking. I deserve it."

He surprised me and extended his hand. "Forget it. I've been there myself."

We asked for a ride to the dispensary. As I staggered back to the basha, I thought about my terrible mistakes and my marvelous copilot. He reminded me of a few fundamentals: if you come in high, land, don't go around. Don't try to fly over thunderstorms on the Hump. Descending from high altitude, keep your engines warm by lowering the landing gear.

He taught me one more thing: overlook the other guy's mistakes.

Carl F. Constein

The Taj Mahal Caper

With exactly three hundred one hours remaining, I was over halfway to that tantalizing seven hundred fifty number. Averaging ninety hours a month, I should hit the mark sometime in June, July at the latest. I pictured myself stateside, running up to Amy and holding her in my arms.

But before I could accumulate more time, I was directed to take a C-46 to Agra in north central India for major repairs. I had mixed feelings. Remembering Gaya, I hoped for the same easygoing stay. And of course I looked forward to visiting that jewel, the Taj Mahal. But I was concerned about missing Hump time. Above all, I wanted to be on my way home by July.

Everything about the base at Agra was first-rate. The CO and his staff were solicitous of us pilots from the airfields of Assam, making of the experience an unexpected R&R. The transient quarters were spacious, permanent tents with brick floors. The food put Chabua's to shame. Best of all, there wasn't a mountain anywhere to be seen, not even a hillock.

The rec officer went out of his way to be helpful. Not really expecting a positive answer, I asked about tennis. What a surprise. He drove me to a club on the other side of the city, where the pro fixed me up with clothes and a racquet. After so long a layoff, it took me a while to get going, but playing -- on a grass court, no less -- did wonders for my spirit.

The staff arranged for us to visit the Taj Mahal and also Fort Agra, a fascinating fortress where the Emperor Shah Jahan ruled in the sixteenth century. I remember giving a young Hindu boy a rupee to dive from the rampart into a moat sixty feet below. I recall the huge chess board laid out in the courtyard. When princely landlords made their annual trek to pay tribute to the Shah, chess was one of their chief diversions. No wonder: the chess pieces were real live girls.

I recall the guide's showing us the secret passageways to the bedrooms of the Shah's three wives: Hindu, Moslem, and Christian. The Christian wife, Mumtaz Mahal, was his favorite. It was for her that he built the glittering marble mausoleum next to the fort. He must have loved her deeply. In the wall of the fort's portico, hundreds of precious stones had been inlaid to reflect their unique images of the ivory-white shrine. From the balcony I watched a more mundane scene -- a funeral cortege proceeding toward the Jumna River and placing their deceased on a funeral pyre.

The Taj is magnificent. After I retired, I traveled to some of the world's most fascinating places, visiting splendorous cathedrals, palaces, gardens, city halls, theaters, and monuments. Standing there in its sublime isolation, the Taj Mahal tops them all.

But the inside of the Taj is less grand. Removing my shoes, I entered and was surprised to see not one but two tombs. The tomb of Mumtaz Mahal is in the very center; the Taj was built to house it. When the Shah died, he was buried beside her, to the left as you enter. The imbalance contrasts starkly with the symmetry of the outside of the tomb.

The next day, lying on my bunk reading, I was startled to hear someone call my name. I turned and saw a guy dressed in shorts and a safari hat. He looked familiar.

"Hey, Constein. How you doin?"

I spotted an F/O bar on his collar. He was one of the unlucky guys in 44-G in Waco who didn't get a commission.

"I remember you," I said, "but I can't think of your name."

"Come on, Constein. Everyone remembers Joe Buloma. What you doin' in Agra?"

"I brought a C-46 here from Chabua for overhaul. How about you?"

"I've been ferryin' L-4s from Karachi to Burma."

We talked awhile about where we'd been and when we expected to get home. Then he said, "After flyin those big C-46s, you'd probably enjoy a ride in a Piper Cub, wouldn't you? Come on, I'll take you up."

Something told me to say no, but I followed him anyway. Sitting there beside the big twin-engine and four-engine transports, Buloma's L-4 was a toy, a joke. This might be fun after all, I mused as I crawled in.

"Here we go," he said as we skipped down the runway. We lifted off, but instead of climbing, he held the Piper level to pick up speed. Then, abruptly, he pulled back hard on the stick and took her up as steep as she'd tolerate. At 3000 feet he showed off his aerobatic skills with loops and spins. I expected this macho exhibition. We flew every way but straight.

We were over the city. He headed north and started letting down in snaky turns. I suspected what was coming next; I'd heard that buzzing was a must in the repertoire of these guys.

Act one was flying beneath the electric lines that ran like wash lines across the fields, probably fifteen feet off the ground. I couldn't actually feel the wheels touching, but we must have been no more than six inches off the ground. It was just the warm-up, I suspected.

My shirt was drenched in sweat, partly from the one hundred-degree heat, but mainly from the jitters.

Off in the distance Buloma spotted peasants working the fields. Act two. "Buzzing these wags is fun," he laughed. He headed their way, gained a thousand feet, then dove straight down like a Stuka bomber, three feet to spare before he pulled up. He laughed fiendishly as he watched the peasants run, throwing down their baskets, hitting the dirt at the last second.

Beads of sweat stood on my forehead. I was scared for the peasants -- and for myself! All that unavoidable danger over the Hump, and now this? Should I tell him I'd had enough? I knew better. I was his captive.

He continued buzzing for what seemed an eternity. Then he said, "Okay, are you ready for the last act?"

Intuitively I knew what was next. I saw the Taj Mahal directly ahead. I prayed his last act wouldn't be mine as well.

When we were a half-mile away, I called out, "No, no, Joe. We can't do this." My shirt was soaked. My hands were wet.

He laughed. "What are you going to do, take over the plane? Relax, there's plenty of room. Hell, you might be famous."

That's what I was afraid of. We were approaching from the south. Thirty seconds away. My heart skipped when I suspected the worst -- he was going to fly not over the dome, but between the dome and the two minarets on the right! I said a quick prayer. Please God, if I have to crash, let it be on the Hump not into the Taj Mahal.

In a second, I looked *up* at the top of the dome. In another second, we were past the Taj, past the danger.

I exhaled loudly and shook my head as we pulled away and crossed the river. I turned and looked back at the Taj, my heart racing. Buloma gazed at me and chuckled. We turned east and headed back to the field.

"I'd let you land my little pet, but I see you're still pretty shook up." He let out a guffaw.

We landed and I walked back to my tent, shaking my head; I knew how lucky I'd been.

In a spell of nostalgia some years later, I reminisced about my incredible Taj incident. Even now the memory provokes an involuntary shaking of my head. How much room was there between the L-4's wing tips and the arcaded kiosks on our left and the minarets on the right?

I remembered Joe Buloma's words: "Plenty of room."

Born to Fly the Hump

Guests of the Maharajah

So far from Europe, V-E Day didn't cause a big stir in Chabua. We were quietly thrilled, but the inevitability of victory after the momentous landings at Normandy toned down any celebration. And there was still Japan. The word we heard was there'd be no Japanese defeat without a bloody invasion of the island, perhaps a million American casualties.

What was I doing on V-E Day? My log for May 8, 1945, shows I flew C-46 number 966 to Luliang, China, seven hours and five minutes, two hours twenty minutes on instruments. All of May, in fact, was a busy month for me in the air, one hundred four hours, fifteen flights, six to Kunming, four to Chanyi, three to Chengkung, two to Luliang, none of them ticked off in my log/notebook as troublesome or eventful.

The monsoon now made its full presence felt. In the early spring, especially on the China end of the Hump, monster thunderheads were a menace. But the trademark of the monsoon was its gray solid overcast, requiring instrument flying through layers of stratus on all flights.

Flying became downright boring: no scenery to savor except a few peaks which peeped through the overcast like turtles, and no vertical clouds to challenge my imagination. At least in fall and winter I could look down through broken clouds to ancient villages sprinkled throughout the jungles and mountainsides. So many tribes, so many cultures, so many languages. What was life like down there?

I looked also for broken fuselages on the 400-plane "aluminum trail," wondering why in seven months on the Hump I hadn't spotted a one. Even on his first Hump flight, General Tunner reported he sighted one. That macho flight as pilot on his first day as CO was fool-hardy, in my opinion, (later he acknowledged this) for he wasn't checked out in a C-46 and knew practically nothing about the route.

But I credit Willie the Whip Tunner with increasing monthly tonnage from 23,000 when he took over in August, 1944, to 70,000 a year later -- and with a reduced accident and loss rate. Still, dangers remained. Between January and March of 1945 (I was in Chabua from the end of October, 1944, through October, 1945) one hundred thirty-four pilots and crew were killed in seventy-seven major accidents. Equating Hump time to combat flying, the Air Corps awarded eighty percent of its decorations in the CBI to Hump pilots. I received the Distinguished Flying Cross and the Air Medal with cluster. But the honors were no great shakes; no ceremony either time. Zilch.

Only one phobia nagged me about flying the Hump -- I always felt a lump in my throat when I was stacked up over a field in China or India, in the soup, on instruments, the tower directing my descent five hundred feet at a time until I became number one to land. My fear was that one of the dozen or so planes holding above me might call a Mayday and come barreling down through the stack unseen, a collision waiting to happen. Three times I found myself in this predicament, each time reacting with a string of prayers. Three times my prayers were heard. Three times my luck held.

A risk none of us considered, a silent risk, was anoxia. At 19,000 feet, how long could we fly without harm if we had an oxygen leak? Bill Spatz, a friend of mine from home who flew C-46s out of Sookerating, unknowingly had a failure like this on one flight. A few years after he was discharged, he developed puzzling ailments difficult to diagnose. Anoxia was the suspect. Bill died a sad death in a VA hospital.

For me, so far so good. Keep your fingers crossed, I told myself. It was June and I began counting down my flights. When my friends Smokey and Murray urged me to go on R&R with them, I didn't immediately say yes, the seven hundred fifty-hour target so much an obsession.

We'd heard about how wonderful Shillong was, not just the town and the people of the Khasi Hills but the quaint hotel and, especially, the princely estate of the Maharajah. He'd graciously turned over his regal playground to servicemen and British civil servants. Every pilot who'd been there raved about this Shangri-la, set like a gem in the dreary Indian countryside two hundred fifty miles southwest of Chabua. I opted to go, and a week later the three of us were on our way, saved-up fifths of whiskey peeping out from our shoulder bags.

An open lorry took us up a winding dirt road to our one-week heaven in the Khasi Hills, an enclave of Indian Christians a mile above sea level. We were struck by their light skin and pleasant demeanor.

We registered and settled into the cozy Fernwood, a picture postcard hotel run by a Swiss couple. It was late afternoon. Hopping into the hotel's lorry, we took a quick trip to town. On the way, I got a glimpse of the Maharajah's lifestyle -- a golf course, eight red clay tennis courts, a race track, a sumptuous club house. The Maharajah's palace was elsewhere in his princely state.

Shillong was as different from Dibrigarugh, the village near Chabua, as an American suburb from a city slum. The main street was paved, shops were orderly and attractive. The vendors smiled, pleased to have us.

Dinner at eight, the desk clerk told us when we walked into the lobby. He added, "People usually meet at seven for drinks."

The three of us had a little drink of our own before joining other guests in a reception area off the dining room. What an attractive company we found ourselves in. Many of the guests were English, about half civilian, half military. A handsome Indian couple looked resplendent in their rich attire. A few Englishmen were dressed in tuxedos, many women in gowns. I believe we had our jackets with us. I hope we did.

Any feeling of discomfort disappeared as soon as we had drinks in our hands. The English guests graciously moved about and engaged all their American cousins in conversation. Time passed quickly; the dinner bell welcomed us.

The food was superb, honest-to-goodness beef, fresh vegetables, scrumptious Swiss pastries and the richest, most delicious peach ice cream on earth. The native waiters were dressed in long robes with cummerbunds and wore turbans and white gloves. This was high life. I did a double take when I caught sight of one waiter who somehow looked familiar. It came to me. My God, I said to my buddies, Hollywood sent its favorite comedian to serve us -- Jerry

Cologna. There he was -- handle-bar mustache, fetching smile and all. We asked that he serve us every night. More with facial expressions and gestures than words, the repartee was unforgettable.

One night we ate with Englishman Tom Parks and his wife. In the Indian Civil Service for twenty years, he was superintendent of a munitions factory outside Calcutta. I liked the Parks immediately. Hard of hearing, he leaned on his wife to carry the conversation. She was a lovely woman, probably in her fifties, sensitive, drawing out of us a bit of our lives back home, thanking us for our service. I wish I could remember her first name.

At our table the next night was a fascinating trio, a retired British colonel and his niece and her girlfriend. Both knockouts, the niece tall, her friend more shapely, the gals were the object of a thousand stares, a thousand longings, and perhaps, in spite of the colonel's tight oversight, a close encounter or two. Overhearing my conversation with Murray about golf, the colonel asked whether his two charges might make it a foursome. They were beginners, it turned out, but a lot of fun.

Years later when I saw *My Fair Lady* the image of the British colonel in Shillong shot into my mind. Colonel Pickering!

The joy of my week was the tennis. Every morning like clockwork, a brief shower struck the area. As soon as it ended, the courts were rolled and brushed. Then two little ball boys dressed in blue shorts and shirts ran unto the court. What a deal! Never before or since have I been so catered to on the tennis court. I played every morning, all morning.

One afternoon we went shopping in town. I bought Amy a beautiful star sapphire for a pittance of rupees. Bill Diller, the jeweler at home who had opened his store for us on a Sunday a year earlier, appraised it at a hundred dollars. I should have bought a pocketful.

The social highlight of the week came on Saturday night when we were all invited to a dance at the Maharajah's magnificent club house. I noticed a whist room down the hallway. There was a handsome walnut bar, a dining room, and a large ballroom. I danced with Mrs. Parks, the two girls, and a few other English ladies.

I had my best time at the bar. I pulled up a stool beside a British officer who appeared to be in his forties and ordered a whiskey. I can't recall the spark that set us off or who started it, but suddenly, after a few drinks we were engrossed in a game of "name that poem."

"Oh, to be in England ..." I threw out.

"Now that April's here," he responded quickly, "and whoever wakes in England ... Robert Browning, of course," he added.

We took turns lining out the challenges. He gave me, "It is a beauteous evening, calm and free ..."

"Wordsworth," I said. "The holy time is quiet as a nun."

The more we drank, the more spirited we became. Some guests semi-circled around us to take in the game. I threw him a curve with an American poet. "And he was rich -- yes, richer than a king -- and admirably schooled in every grace."

"Ah," the major said, "I know it. American. Give me a little more."

"... In fine, we thought that he was everything to make us wish that we were in his place."

"I'm getting there. Yes, yes, I've got it," he said with a big smile. "That's old Richard Cory in Edgar Lee Master's *Spoon River Anthology.*"

The poetry romp was a grand finale to a week I've never forgotten. We left for Chabua the next day, each of us with a pocketful of memories, if not sapphires.

The Whole Tooth

Back in Chabua, I went around in a semi daze, my mind fixed on Shillong. Snap out of it, I told myself; time to get back to work. A hundred fifty more hours, twenty some flights, and I'm out of here. I went to bed tired but happy.

Two days later I was on my way to China. It took forever for Dumbo to get there, it seemed, even longer to return to India. Einstein's law of relativity was at work. I made nine more trips in June, none of them eventful, but each one feeling longer than the last. I did a lot of squirming in the cockpit. Once in bed, I had a hard time falling asleep. I wrote to my wife every other day now.

July finally crept in, a month I'd hoped would be my last on the Hump. One night, sleeping fitfully, I awoke with a start, pain like a hot wire shooting into a back tooth. I paced the floor. Counting the hours, I waited anxiously for 0800 then rushed to the dispensary.

I recall the dentist chair, a nineteenth century torture chamber. "You won't need this wisdom tooth," the young captain said. "I'll give you a shot of Novocain and pull it."

Removing the culprit turned out to be a struggle. I wondered how many teeth he'd pulled in his brief career. Finally, with one last grunt, he yanked it out, blood gushing from the hole. I exhaled loudly and fell back.

"Want to take it along as a memento?" he asked after he'd stopped the bleeding. When I got up to leave, he said, "I'm going to ground you till your mouth heals. Come back in four days and I'll check it."

Ambling back to the basha, I was troubled. So close to the magic mark, I felt uneasy. I prayed there'd be no last-minute hitch.

After four days of pacing like a caged tiger, I hoofed it to the dispensary. The dentist put me back on flight status, and I was raring to go. Returning from a late breakfast, I spotted a crowd of guys around the bulletin board.

"What's going on?" I asked Foley.

"That bastard Tunner really did it to us this time," he said.

"What do you mean? What did he do?"

"The son of a bitch came up with a new order -- everyone stays a year!"

"Oh no," I moaned. "I just missed it!"

I staggered away in a daze. For one lousy tooth I'd languish in India three interminable months. And after I finish flying, what will I be doing then? I trudged to the basha, gulped down a shot of whiskey, and lay on the bunk. Okay, get hold of yourself, I said. One thing at a time. First, get your seven hundred fifty hours. The date was July 8 -- I had exactly fifty-one hours twenty minutes to go.

If June seemed a poky month, July was snail like. I couldn't believe how long my flights took, twice as long, it seemed, as my early Hump trips. The monsoon was in its prime, and fighting the ice kept me plenty busy, but even so, the clock on the instrument panel always lagged on behind. Don't complain, I told myself; your flights have been going well.

Finally, almost unbelievably, came my personal V Day, the day I'd dreamed about for nine months. The date was July 28. I was slated for Kunming. Three weeks earlier I'd made a big time chart and hung it on the wall between Rita Hayworth and Betty Grable. After every flight I'd rushed back to the basha to bring my record up to date. I double-checked my arithmetic.

Flight	Date	Hours	Remaining
89	July 8	8:40	51:20
90	July 10	7:30	44:50
91	July 13	6:55	37:55
92	July 16	9:30	27:25
93	July 19	8:10	19:15
94	July 21	7:00	12:15
95	July 24	7:10	5:05
96	?	?	BINGO!

So here I was, my last day on the Hump. The morning was dreary, completely overcast. I filed a flight plan and we got a lift to our plane. Number 280 looked brand new, silver, not the ugly gray-brown camouflage of most C-46s. I gave it an admiring look as I walked around and inspected for cuts in the tires and leaks under the engine nacelles. Everything had to be perfect today.

I motioned for the copilot to call the tower. The engines started easily and I taxied to the end of the runway. The mags checked okay. A bit jittery, I lined up with the runway and shoved the throttles home. We lifted off at exactly 0800.

We were in the weather a second after takeoff. We climbed normally over Moran, headed out on the Easy route and got on top of the monsoon ceiling at 16,500 feet. The sun was brilliant. My head was on a swivel, checking for any planes straying off course. So far, so good -- no turbulence, just a little ice.

At 1055 hours the radio compass needle did its 180. Kunming tower directed us to hold in the stack. Please, God, no Mayday above me today. In twenty-five minutes we were safely on the ground. We'd logged three hours twenty minutes. That left two hours, thirty-five minutes to go. I'd be in the very middle of the Hump when my time was up. Not an apt phrase, I mused. Change it to -- when I reached the goal. Even thoughts had to be perfect today.

I made a smooth landing, taxied to the line, and shut down. We checked into operations then went next door for my last "Flied Eck-ges, Cho" and bread, still the best meal on the Hump. I gave the Chink who served me a Ding Hao.

After eating, I paced around operations like a roiled CEO. The copilot, with whom I'd flown before, said, "You seem a bit jumpy. Anything wrong?"

I shared my happy secret, and we climbed into the waiting jeep. In ten minutes we were airborne, heading west. Go west, young man, go west. Four more hours. I said a silent prayer after we got to altitude and I threw on the automatic pilot. My mind wandered -- to home, as always, but also to several close calls. I prayed again. Please God, no more close calls. No more trouble. Not today. Both engines purred like kittens. I smiled.

We'd taken off at 1330; it was now 1600. I peered through a break in the overcast and there, just as I had calculated on my prehistoric government-issue E6-B "computer" was the east branch of the Irrawaddy River meandering through the jungle. The jungle looked peaceful.

Five minutes passed. I yanked off my mask, nudged the copilot, and smiled broadly. "You are looking at one happy guy. Right now, at this minute, my log shows seven hundred fifty hours."

"Congratulations," he said, "but you'd better hold the champagne till we're on the ground. I'll buy you a drink -- at the dispensary." He chuckled.

An hour and ten minutes to touchdown, I figured. Even at altitude, I felt hot, my palms sweating.

At 7000 feet, ten minutes out, I called the tower. This final time I wanted to do it myself. "Victor George, this is 127. Request landing instructions. Over."

"Roger, 127. Hold over the beacon at 7000 feet."

Again I mused -- please, no Maydays today. "Roger. I thought you might like to know. I've just reached seven hundred fifty hours."

No response.

I was soaked when we finally got through the stack and landed. Again, smooth as silk. Cautiously, I taxied to the revetment, shut off the engines and pulled out my notebook and pencil. "Flight 96, July 28, C-46 127 to Kunming, 7 hours, 30 minutes, 2:10 instruments." I gave it extra space in the notebook and circled it twice. Walking on air, I sauntered to the basha, whistling Mozart.

Unable to contain my happiness at dinner, I prattled on in small talk. One guy gave me a funny look. Ambling back to the basha, I switched my tune to Beethoven's "Ode to

Joy." I sat and immediately wrote to Amy, giving her the sensational news that I was at last finished flying the Hump, adding, unhappily, that I had to stay in Chabua for three more months -- all because a wisdom tooth acted up and grounded me for four days.

That tooth loomed so large in my thoughts I wanted to save it, so I sent it home. What Amy was looking for was something beautiful, something precious. Imagine her shock when she unwrapped the tiny package and saw -- not a precious gem, not the star sapphire she so eagerly anticipated, but a big, ugly tooth! I never heard the end of that.

It took me a week to get over my bad luck of missing the "750 hours and home" regulation by just a few days. Exactly what would they do with me for three months? It seems incredible, but the brass apparently hadn't considered that when they issued the new order of a one-year tour of duty. The right way, the wrong way, and the Army way.

During this twilight period, I sat around and did nothing. On August first I pulled the duty of tower officer of the day. It was indeed a big day -- Army Air Force Day. Rather than taking General Arnold's recommendation that all commands celebrate through parades or open-houses, General Tunner took a different tack. August first would be a day of work as usual on the Hump, except that the one-day tonnage record would be challenged. Tunner insisted that all personnel be involved.

It worked. At the end of the day, the Command had flown a thousand one hundred-eighteen round trips, a plane crossing the Hump every minute and twelve seconds, over five thousand tons carried. Tunner himself flew three round-trips during the twenty-four-hour period.

And what did the officer of the day think of all this hoopla? Not much. I agreed with General Tunner that so close to Japan it was inappropriate to celebrate. But the one-day push was artificial, theatrical. Besides, the end was in sight; the Hump would soon be phased out. But who knows? Perhaps an effort like this was in Tunner's memory bank when, three years later, he commanded the Berlin Airlift so brilliantly.

Two weeks later we heard news that shocked the world. The Enola Gay had dropped a powerful mystery bomb on Hiroshima. After a second atomic strike three days later, this one on Nagasaki, Japan surrendered. What was I doing on V-J Day, August 14, 1945? Finished with the Hump, I was flying to Agra. Valley time like this went toward the four hours I needed for monthly flight pay.

I spent my twenty-fifth birthday in Agra revisiting the Taj, this time more relaxed, and touring the city. After the overhaul of the C-46 was finished, I prepared to leave. In operations I overheard the dispatcher say he needed someone to deliver a partial cargo to Calcutta. I volunteered to drop it off on my return to Chabua and immediately called the Parks. Mrs. Parks was delighted to hear from me and invited my copilot and me to visit. She said Tom would pick us up at Dum Dum Field.

My visit to their home was an eye-opener -- large and richly furnished, complete with a cook, a waiter, and two other servants. We enjoyed a scrumptious dinner and a wonderful evening.

After the war, about a year after India won its self-rule from England, I heard from the Parks, now back in England. The letter was depressing. After many years of living high as civil servants in India, they had a painful adjustment to their meager lifestyle and the social changes that had taken place in England.

When I got back to Chabua, I learned that all pilots who had their time in were given two choices -- continue flying the Hump or take a new assignment. No one in his right mind would choose the first option. Besides, the Hump was closing down. Why would that even be an option?

I thought I caught a break. For the first time in the service, I was offered an assignment I was qualified for -- assistant training officer. I knew there'd be no serious training, but still ....

A few days later I walked into a small office at the end of the flight line and reported to the training officer. Except for two desks and chairs, the office was bare, not even a phone or a file cabinet. I introduced myself, and before the captain laid it out, I got the picture. We'd been sent to Siberia. Report every day -- and do absolutely nothing!

The captain was a character. After awhile we tired of reading, and we ran out of things to talk about. But he always had one subject to discuss, the obsession on the lips of GIs the world over -- sex. Embarrassingly, he fantasized aloud about the adventures he planned, down to the number of times per week.

"Martin Luther considered twice a week proper," I told him, smiling, knowing he wouldn't accept that.

"Thank God I'm not Lutheran," he said, bursting out laughing.

Two more months of boredom. I recalled two earlier stretches of agony. Which was worse -- cutting ticking in a mattress factory, guarding coal piles with a gun on my shoulder, or this? Ennui blended with happiness: I was alive, I'd soon be home!

Going Home

Home! Every single day for nearly a year I dreamed of home. On some flights over the Hump, cruising on automatic pilot, I thought of nothing else. My heart longed for home.

In late October, almost exactly to the year, orders were cut for me to report to Camp Shanks, New York. Gladly! I must have read my copy fifteen times. Poe, Peterson, and two other buddies and I were moved out of our basha and billeted in a tent in the old polo grounds. The monsoon had just ended its half-year stay, leaving the transient area a sea of mud.

For some men, going home was so strong an obsession it affected their reasoning. Unwilling to stay in Chabua even one more day, they chose to travel across India on the Assam-Bengal Cannonball Express -- crowded, dirty, snail-paced. Along the way, passengers had to transfer to another train several times when the tracks switched gauges. These guys arrived in Karachi a week after the flight they couldn't wait for.

We boarded a C-54 for Karachi, that steaming hellhole so vivid in my memory. Knowing I'd soon be on my way home, I could put up with anything, I mused.

My two best Hump friends, Smokey and Murray, showed up one day. I was happy to see them, of course, but

I was also upset. They'd arrived in Chabua three months after I had, but they were going home at the same time I was. Actually, before me, it turned out. Two days later they boarded a DC-4 for the states while I languished in Karachi for another ten days.

Not everyone was going to fly home. It was the luck of the draw -- three weeks by ship, less than half that by plane. I didn't feel lucky. I was right. I had only a day to get myself set for a long sea voyage. I dashed off a letter to Amy, telling her I'd arrive in New York around December 7 on the 20,000-ton Norwegian freighter M.S Torrens. I told her to check the arrivals in the New York Times.

I recall few details about my passage to a new life. I remember I slept on the top bunk of five, the sardine on top of the can, perhaps three inches between me and the deck above. The mattresses looked like the ones I cut at the Fleetwood Craftsmen, probably were.

Out in the Arabian Sea, the weather was pleasant, warm enough for us to spend our days on deck, and the sea was calm. We were sailing in a southwesterly direction. Unless you were a gambler or a card shark, loafing or reading were the pastimes. I was halfway through Kipling's *The Light That Failed* when a buddy hailed me. Turning, I knocked the book overboard and watched it slowly sink to the bottom of the sea. Funny the things you remember.

The Torrens entered the Gulf of Aden and turned northwesterly into the Red Sea, the weather and the sea still calm. Everyone grew excited as we neared the Suez Canal. The captain told us to watch for Egypt's King Farouk's yacht, docked somewhere off to the starboard. We approached Port Said and sailed into the Mediterranean. From there to New York it was due west.

The Mediterranean was even calmer than the Arabian Sea and the Red Sea. Setting us up for something, I mused. One distinct memory I have is of sitting on a gun platform on moonlight nights on the Mediterranean. "It was a beauteous evening, calm and free." My mind went back to the poetry caper in Shillong.

We were at sea about two weeks when we sailed past the rock of Gibraltar. The ship's crew knew, even if we didn't, we were about to face the fierce winter storms of the North Atlantic. As though a switch was thrown, the calm seas turned angry. The Torrens rose and fell in the tallest swells any of us had ever imagined. Within an hour I became seasick and remained sick all the way to New York. I couldn't eat, I didn't sleep much, I spent my days at the rail. Even the crew was sick. We heard that the troop ship that left Karachi ahead of us lost its rudder and had to be towed to New York. Looking back, I count those five days the most miserable of my life, worse even than my Dixie Belle misadventure.

At long last, twenty-two days after setting sail, we came into New York harbor in the middle of the night and docked at Staten Island. It was December 7. We debarked and boarded the ferry. It wasn't until I set foot in Manhattan that I felt it -- I was home!

I heard music. There in kilts and full regalia was a Scottish bagpipe band, perhaps forty, piping their welcome. It was two in the morning. Unbelievable. I got goose bumps. Did they greet all troop ships, or was the fourth anniversary of Pearl Harbor a special occasion? It was one of those unexpected special joys that remain with you **always.**

I was amazed at how smoothly everything was going. Why couldn't the Army have shown the same efficiency when the war was on? We boarded a troop train for Camp Shanks, north of New York City, and at five in the morning ate the breakfast of a lifetime -- steak, eggs, and ice cream, in the good old USA! We were treated courteously, respectfully, as though someone really owed us something.

After breakfast I called Amy. She was overjoyed to hear my voice, not altogether surprised because she'd seen in the newspaper the Torrens was scheduled to arrive on time. I told her I'd be discharged from Fort Indiantown Gap, and I asked her to reserve a room in the Harrisburger Hotel.

Able to stretch out on a real bed, exhausted, contented, I had a great night's sleep at Camp Shanks. Early the next morning, I boarded a troop train for Harrisburg. I recall so well how delighted I was to see again those things I'd taken for granted -- sidewalks, lush lawns, pretty houses.

The warmhearted treatment of Camp Shanks continued at Indiantown Gap. Perhaps the Army Air Force was fearful of losing all its pilots. They gave us a deal: take an extra 30-day paid leave, go home, and consider reenlisting for another year. No commitment. If you decide not to, there'll be no pressure. What you gain is one extra month's pay. We didn't trust the buggers: no one took the offer. With accrued leave, my discharge was effective January 13, 1946.

The moment I entered the lobby of the Harrisburger Hotel, I spotted Amy. I rushed to her, threw my arms around her and kissed her passionately. In the life of a young married couple, could there ever be a happier, more glorious moment than this -- safe, together. Nothing would stop us now.

I recall how nervous I felt in the dining room that night. The table next to ours seemed too close. My face and neck felt hot. I felt eyes staring at me. Were people puzzled by my complexion, yellow from a year of taking atabrine to ward off malaria?

Two days later Amy and I left for home in Uncle Carl's Pontiac. I drove. On the highway, cars passed us as though we were standing still.

"Why are they driving so fast?" I asked Amy. By the time we arrived in Reading, I had it figured out. My only driving in the last year was the slow and cautious taxiing of a C-46.

I'd have some readjusting to do. I'd have to learn again to be a civilian.

Epilogue

Fifty-four years have flown by since that night so vivid in my memory when I stepped off the M.S. Torrens onto the dock in Staten Island. I've made the readjustment to highway speeds and to a myriad civilian ways. I've had a full, happy life and a rewarding career in education, first as English teacher, then, after a doctorate at Temple University, as curriculum director, and finally school superintendent.

In my memories, sometimes in my dreams, I've been back on the Hump. I think about the legends of the CBI -- the Flying Tigers, Clair Chennault, Merrill's Marauders, Wingate's Raiders, the redoubtable Vinegar Joe Stilwell, the Fourteenth Air Force. From high above I look down on the serpentine Burma Road, and I imagine myself piloting a huge airplane, flying over the highest mountains and the thickest jungles. Was that me?

My most vivid and sustained memory of the Hump came in 1970. With school superintendents from across the country, I visited the Soviet Union on a three-week study-tour of Soviet education. After a few days in Leningrad (now, again, St. Petersburg) we flew to Tbilisi, capital of the Georgian Republic, in a twin-engine Russian plane, its size and shape eerily like my old C-46. Crossing the Caucasus Mountains, I looked down at the snowcapped peaks. For forty minutes I was back on the Hump, seeing again those breathtaking Himalayas, cringing at the terror of close calls. It was a profound experience.

In the big picture, were any of the legends, any of the heroics in the CBI and on the Hump of consequence? Did any of it mean anything? Of course no one dreamed a mysterious new weapon would obviate a ground invasion of Japan; we thought we needed China for that eventuality.

We owe China our gratitude for tying up over a million Japanese troops which could not then fight us. Without the logistic and moral support of the CBI effort, including the Hump, it is likely that China would have fallen to the Japanese.

In the CBI theater, only the Hump had lasting significance. It was the birthplace of mass strategic airlifts, so vital in Berlin in 1948 and two years later in Korea.

So far from home, I often felt abandoned there in India. But our service was not completely anonymous. Speaking before the House of Commons, British Prime Minister Winston Churchill said, "This incredible feat of transport at 20,000 feet in the air, over ground where engine failure means certain death to the pilot, has been performed by a grand effort which the USA has made in their passionate desire to aid in the resistance of China. Certainly no more prodigious example of strength, science, and organization in this class of work has ever been seen or dreamt of."

Do I have any regrets? How could I? I visited renowned cities and world-famous sites. I walked in strange cultures. I saw mountain beauty most people can never even imagine. I learned a great deal. I had a chance to prove myself. Most of all, I came back whole and sound to a beautiful and loving wife, impatient to start living.

No regrets at all? Maybe one. I flew into China ninety-six times, but I was never once allowed to visit a Chinese city.

Carl F. Constein

About the Author

Dr. Carl Frey Constein is a former school superintendent and education writer. Born in 1920 in Fleetwood, Pennsylvania, a child of what Tom Brokaw has popularized as "The Greatest Generation," he lived through the Depression then faced the century's other great period -- World War Two. He was inducted into the Army in 1943, transferred to the Air Corps, and received his pilot's wings and second lieutenant's commission in August, 1944, at Waco, Texas. He was sent to eastern India to fly cargo to China in C-46s. For his 750 hours flight time on the Hump he was awarded two Air Medals and the Distinguished Flying Cross. Facing danger and tough decisions in flight was, he believes, superb preparation for running a school district, especially during the turmoil of the Sizzling Sixties.

Dr. Constein received his doctorate at Temple University. He has traveled widely and enjoys music and the performing arts, tennis, bridge, and golf. He lives near Reading in Berks County, Pennsylvania.